IDEOLOGY AFTER

THE FALL OF COMMUNISM

DEDICATION

For David Collins

With love

BRIEFINGS is a new series of short books to explain and clarify complex contemporary subjects, written for the non-specialist by experts in their fields. Themes and topics covered will include Feminism, Education, Cosmology, Medical Ethics, Political Ideology, Structuralism, Quantum Physics and Comparative Religion among others.

IDEOLOGY AFTER THE FALL OF COMMUNISM

The triumph of liberal democracy?

Peter Collins

BRIEFINGS
Series Editor: Peter Collins

BOYARS/BOWERDEAN
LONDON. NEW YORK

First published in 1993 jointly by the Bowerdean Publishing Co. Ltd.
of 55 Bowerdean St., London, SW6 3TN and Marion Boyars Publishers of
24 Lacy Rd., London SW15 1NL and 237 East 39th St., New York, NY 10016.

Distributed in Australia by Peribo Pty Ltd., Terrey Hills, NSW 2084.

The **BRIEFINGS** series is the property of the Bowerdean Publishing Co. Ltd.

A CIP catalogue record for this book is available from the British Library.

A CIP catalog record for this book is available from the Library of Congress.

ISBN 0 7145 2971 0 Original Paperback.

Designed and typeset by the Bowerdean Publishing Co. Ltd.
Printed and bound in Great Britain by Itchen Printers Ltd., Southampton.

CONTENTS

ACKNOWLEDGEMENT

I take this opportunity of expressing my thanks to the University of Cape Town for material and moral support in the production of this volume and in connection with the editing of the Briefings series as a whole.

Peter Collins
Department of Political Studies
University of Cape Town
RONDEBOSCH
Cape Town
Republic of South Africa

PREFACE

This book is intended as a teaching tool for use especially by those who wish to teach themselves. As such it aspires to make available basic information about what the various ideological "-isms" which are discussed here really mean and what *arguments* can best be used both in their favour and against them.

However, because the object of the exercise is to get people not only to understand but also to be able to develop and engage in arguments, I have attempted to propose and provoke such arguments as well as simply presenting them. Consequently, this book articulates a specific and no doubt controversial thesis about the future of ideology after Communism and the claim that, in some sense, the end of the Cold War constituted not only a bloodless victory in the material domain for the West over the Communist Bloc: it also constitutes a decisive vindication of the ideology of liberal democracy against what had previously been its most powerful rival for the intellectual and emotional allegiance of human beings everywhere. In advancing my thesis about this a number of subsidiary claims are made about individual ideologies which are also open to dispute.

This goes against the pedagogic orthodoxy which holds that teaching texts should strive to be neutral about ideological matters. Such a proposal seems to me not only impracticable but also educationally unsound since it commits the fallacy which Kirkegaard somewhere identifies as follows: "To think about the problems of existence in such a way as to leave out the passion is tantamount to not thinking about them at all. For it is to forget the crucial fact that the thinker himself is an existing and passionate human being."

I have therefore sought to offer clear views, sometimes quite forcefully expressed, whose cogency readers may then assess for themselves and which I hope they will argue about and against, whether or not they end up by accepting them.

Needless to say, I think the theses I offer are true and of some importance but that is less important than that the material from which they emerge should be intelligible, informative and interesting.

CHAPTER ONE

INTRODUCTION

Uncannily, the Fall of the Bastille and the Fall of the Berlin Wall are separated by almost exactly two hundred years. Both events and their dates are profoundly symbolic. July 14th, 1789, and November 10th, 1989, mark moments of revolutionary climax in which a wide and widespread variety of forces for change converged to sweep away, finally and irrevocably, the old order.

In both cases the old order was identified as tyrannical and the promised new order was to be characterised by freedom and justice after years of cruel, capricious, corrupt and incompetent despotism. But neither event is to be understood solely in terms of a struggle for political power in which the oppressed masses finally triumphed over their oppressors. For it was ideas as much as, or even more than institutions which were overthrown and replaced; and these ideas permeated the whole of life, not only the realm of politics. For a proper assessment of these revolutions, therefore, we need to understand not only the events that occurred in the course of the drama but also the convictions of the individuals and groups who participated in the action.

Clearly, we have entered here into the domain of ideology, in at least one fundamental sense of that term. This is the sense in which "ideology" refers to any set of beliefs which apparently determine behaviour over some broad area of human activity — political conduct, economic endeavour, artistic creation or religious practice.

In the French case, absolutist monarchical government was violently destroyed as were the traditional powers and privileges of the aristocracy and the clergy. In the case of the revolution or revolutions in the former Soviet Empire, Communist rule in all its forms was overwhelmingly (but with surprisingly little violence so far) discredited and discarded. In both cases it was not just that a particular government became no longer capable

1

of governing and could thus be expelled from power by opponents. The whole *system of government* collapsed and with it the whole *system of beliefs* with which it had been associated. These beliefs constituted the ruling ideology which the ruling elite sought to impose on all those who were ruled and it encompassed the realms of the philosophical, the religious, the cultural, the social and the economic as well as the straightforwardly political. Indeed, it is the fact that the events of 1789 and 1989 penetrated all aspects of human thought, action and experience that made them genuinely revolutionary. And in the case of the French Revolution the proof that they did so is to be found by examining what went before and what came after[1].

In terms which are no doubt too crude, in France the ideas and ideals which culminated in, and prevailed after the Revolution were those of liberalism, nationalism and imperialism in politics, of capitalism in economics, of Romanticism in culture and of secularism in religion. The norms and beliefs which were central to these "-isms" overlapped and entered into a variety of combinations with one another. Romantic sensibility fuelled nationalist passions; liberalism's emphasis on individual freedom reinforced and was reinforced by arguments for capitalist economic arrangements; and all of these "-isms" impacted on traditional understandings of religion, but were also to a greater or lesser degree shaped by reaction to those understandings.

Before the French Revolution the dominant "-isms" in France were — again speaking very roughly — absolutism in politics, feudalism in economics, neo-classicism in art, and Roman Catholicism in religion. And it was the beliefs which composed these bodies of doctrine which were challenged and largely defeated by the revolutionaries. It is important to say "largely" here because, as we shall see, one of the strongest objections to talking about history in ideological terms is that such talk drastically oversimplifies the realities; and it is of course not true that the French

1. I spell "Communist" with a capital "C" when referring to actual regimes, parties, institutions etc. and the ideology they officially espouse; with a small "c" when referring to the theory of communism, as most notably expounded by Karl Marx and his followers. Similarly for other ideological terms such as "liberal," "socialist" and "conservative."

Revolution can be adequately understood simply as a war between the values and institutions of the Old and New Regimes in which the latter triumphed and the former perished. The conflict between conservatives and radicals persisted throughout the nineteenth century in France, with the conservatives on the "Right" championing precisely the cause of the Monarchy, the landed Aristocracy and the Church, while the radicals on the "Left"[2] were developing and transforming the liberal doctrines of the Enlightenment into various schools of Socialism.

Moreover, and still more importantly from the point of view of learning lessons for our own times from the history of past events, the French Revolution notoriously culminated initially, not in an era of liberty, equality and fraternity but in tyranny and terror at least as brutal as that which had preceded it. It also led, after the Reign of Terror under Robespierre, to Napoleon's dictatorship and the Napoleonic wars which ravaged Europe and led to the Restoration of the Monarchy after the defeat of France in 1815. Concomitantly, the ideological doctrines of the Revolutionaries came to be seen by many as both wrong and repugnant while the convictions of the Reactionaries, who wanted to go back to the way things were, were greatly fortified.

All this raises the question: "And what will happen now, after the fall of Communism in the erstwhile Soviet Union and amongst its former satellites?" More specifically, it raises such questions as: "Will the formerly Communist world now become Capitalist, liberal and democratic in its institutions and ideals?" "If not, will Communist theory and practice be replaced by some other totalitarian and tyrannical regime, for example, neo- or quasi-Fascist dictatorship?" "Or might there even be a reversion to old-style Communism?" "Or perhaps, after all, there will now finally emerge a new and true version of communism which will repudiate the travesties of Lenin and Stalin and at last do justice, in every sense of the phrase, to Karl Marx's great and humane vision?" Other questions about ideology also force themselves on our attention in this connection such as "Where does

2. The terms "Right" and "Left" in their modern political sense were coined just before the French Revolution to distinguish between those who, in the Assembly Chamber of the Estates-General, sat on the left of the King and opposed him from those who sat on his right and supported him.

3

nationalism fit into the picture?" "What about religious fundamentalism of various sorts?" and "Are we, perhaps, now entering an era which will be free of all ideology?"

These questions hinge on, and inevitably provoke others such as: "Is communism now irrevocably discredited as an ideology?" "If not, how much of it, can be rescued and how?" "If so, what ideological convictions and commitments, if any, will replace it in the hearts and minds of people and of peoples?"

The answers to these questions are clearly of crucial importance for anticipating and planning for future events which will affect the lives of everyone. They bear directly on a number of awesome concrete questions which the collapse of Communism has forced the whole world to confront. These include: "What is going to happen to nuclear weapons and the technology for manufacturing them now that there is no cold war between two super-powers to ensure that both the weapons and their manufacturers are kept under the tightest possible control?" "What are the economic implications for the First World and the Third World of the fact that the Second World has disintegrated into paupery?" "Who in this fallen and fragmented empire will now come to power, where and with what consequences?" "What will be the impact of these momentous upheavals on Europe, on the one hand, and Asia, on the other?" etc.

From these considerations it should be clear that apparently abstract ideological questions are inseparable from obviously concrete and practical ones. To try to foresee events which are likely to occur in the world of persons as opposed to the world of things necessitates trying to discern what people are likely to think, to feel and to want. Consequently, anticipating in the domain of human conduct is not like predicting in the natural sciences, because how human beings behave, both individually and collectively, is substantially determined by their beliefs, sentiments and desires, which is not true of the behaviour of atoms and asteroids. Moreover, these "mental states" are not brute and immutable facts about people, like the colour of their eyes or their blood type: rather, they are changeable and capable of being consciously moulded by intelligent reflection, deliberation and discussion. To anticipate what is going to happen to people in the future, therefore, means in part, trying to foresee what people are likely to decide to do. This in turn requires an examination of both the subjective, psychological persuasiveness and the objective, rational cogency of the ideological arguments which, one way or another, will present themselves.

For this reason a study of ideological arguments cannot be neutral since, of necessity, it requires consideration, not only of what people in fact believe and want, but also of what there are good reasons for people to believe and want. This short book is centrally concerned with the future ideological commitments and convictions which are likely to dominate the politics of different parts of the world and of international relations now that Communism has apparently collapsed. This central task, however, which is about matters of empirical fact, is logically flanked by two others, a preliminary one about the meaning of terms and a subsequent one about values.

It is a mistake to think that probing questions about the meanings of words is either easy or trivial. As we shall see, it is very difficult to develop a clear and accurate account of what can most usefully be understood by such terms as "liberalism" and "socialism," "communism" and "capitalism," "democratism" and "elitism," "fundamentalism" and "secularism," etc. Certainly it is by no means easy to make the difficulties involved easily understood. This is particularly true of ideological language where the dangers of deception and self-deception are particularly virulent and it is this that makes the ruthless pursuit of clarity and rigour in the use of ideological language not merely intellectually attractive but of vital practical importance.[3] For in analysing ideological terminology we are analysing the ideas which that terminology is used (or abused) to express and those ideas impel and impassion moral, political and religious behaviour.

---

3. One extremely forceful articulation of this claim is to be found in George Orwell's essay "Politics and the English Language". He writes: " Political language — and with variations this is true of all political parties, from Conservatives to Anarchists — is designed to make lies sound truthful and murder respectable, and to give an appearance of solidity to pure wind." (*Shooting an Elephant*, New York, Harcourt Brace, (1945) p.92).

For all its difficulty and importance, trying to analyse ideas of the sort involved in ideological language — an endeavour which is partly historical and partly philosophical in character — is less daunting than attempting to anticipate the ideas which will be widely prevalent in the future. This latter task is of necessity speculative and, if it is not to degenerate into mere guesswork requires, in addition to being scrupulously clear about what one is talking about, a consideration of what people are likely to believe, both for good reasons and for bad. This takes us into territory where the studies of psychology and of ethics cohabit and are not always easy to distinguish. It is a territory in which we are compelled to *evaluate* ideological claims and commitments in terms of both their reasonableness and — what is, of course, by no means the same thing — their power to persuade. Value-judgments, however, are not to be equated with simple prejudices or "mere" personal opinions. They are also capable of being supported and criticised on the basis of rational argument and, where the future of ideology is concerned, how people reason about values will crucially shape what they come to believe and how they choose to behave.

All these considerations have to be taken into account when trying to assess the likely development of ideological thinking subsequent to the events surrounding November 10, 1989. However, to give focus to what might otherwise be an unduly amorphous treatment, this short book concentrates on the view that the collapse of Communism has signalled the final ideological triumph of liberal democratism (or democratic liberalism) so that the principles and practices of this ideology have finally come to be decisively vindicated against their principal rival and may now be expected to gain ever widerspread acceptance throughout the world.

I call this view about the supposedly irreversible triumph of liberal democracy the "TOLD" thesis. It is closely related to the so-called "End-of-Ideology" thesis and has been recently articulated as a response to the collapse of Communism under the name "the end-of-History" thesis. The TOLD thesis constitutes a natural starting-point for an inquiry into the future of ideology after Communism for four reasons. First, it is at once the simplest and most drastic intellectual response to the collapse of

Communism, since it postulates (if not always explicitly) the inevitable and universal triumph of Western ideology and, with it, the triumph of reason and goodness over folly and evil. Secondly, this thesis has seemed to offer the most obvious explanation of recent global events to the general public as well as to many professional students of politics. Thirdly, a consideration of the view that the triumph of liberal democracy has put an end to the need for further ideological disputation, forces us to consider carefully the nature and meaning of ideology in general. Fourthly, it is a thesis whose central components — the doctrines of democracy and of liberalism — are much less clearly understood than is popularly assumed, as are the principal arguments which have been adduced both for and against them.

Consequently, apart from trying to assess the cogency of the TOLD thesis itself, the main purpose of this book is expository. It is to equip interested readers with some of the conceptual tools, the factual information and the evaluative arguments which will enable them to form their own judgments about ideological matters. It is true that in the course of this enterprise I am bound to express and seek to defend ideological commitments and convictions of my own. Some of these may not only be disputed: they may also give offence. This is not intentional but it is probably an inevitable consequence of dealing with the kinds of belief by which people try to live, for which often they fight and for which, sometimes, they are prepared to die. On the other hand, I obviously hope that some of the considerations I adduce in support of my views may strike some readers as persuasive. Either way, the object of this book will have been achieved if, by considering arguments both for and against the views I express, readers are enabled to form a clearer and more cogent grasp of the ideological position to which they choose to give their own allegiance.

CHAPTER TWO
IDEOLOGY AND THE END
OF IDEOLOGY

One possible and radical answer to the question: "What will be the ideological future of the world now that Soviet Communism has collapsed?" is that there won't be one. And there won't be one because the triumph of the "West"[1] in the Cold War has eliminated the conditions which make the articulation and propagation of any ideology necessary.

This view lies at the heart of the so-called "End-of-History thesis" as it has been recently revived, popularised and applied by the American political scientist, Francis Fukuyama. The thesis itself goes back to the work of the profound, but often profoundly obscure nineteenth century German philosopher, G.W.F. Hegel. It is also closely related to the "end-of-ideology thesis" which flourished in America in the 1950's and which also held that communism is a spent moral and political force and, consequently, there are now no further grounds for ideological conflict

1. The "West" is, of course, a misnomer since it often or usually includes Australasia in the South and Japan in the East. It is, however, sufficiently understood to constitute serviceable shorthand for referring to those countries which are multi-party representative democracies and which are hostile to any form of Command or centrally directed economy. In the same way it is strictly inaccurate to speak of the "East", which in the context of discussion about the end of ideology will be used to refer to the those countries where Communism has recently collapsed, as well as to China where, officially, it has not. The end-of-ideology thesis, in its end-of-History version, foresees that (capitalist) liberal democracy will come to be the dominant ideology, not only in the East, thus defined, but throughout the East, including the Middle East.

8

and hence no further need for intellectual disputation about ideological matters. Before considering the substance of these doctrines as they relate to the question of how we can best understand the allegedly post-Communist and post-communist world which we now inhabit, it is necessary to address the very general question of what ideology is.

The word "ideology" has come to have many meanings since the coinage of its French equivalent by Destutt de Tracy at the time of the French Revolution. Nevertheless, for our purposes, it ought to be enough to distinguish two main kinds of usage.

The first is the older one, associated with de Tracy and the project of the European Enlightenment, in which the etymological meaning of "ideology" as simply the study of ideas becomes focussed on the ideas which animate human conduct especially in the domain of the moral, the political and the religious. This study of what people have believed about these matters, and why, leads on naturally to a consideration of what people ought to believe about them on the basis of evidence and rational argument. And that inquiry turns out to require an attempt at generating a *comprehensive and coherent account of the human condition as a whole; in particular of what, as a matter of fact it is, what it can and should become and what must be done to make it as good as it can be for individuals, for societies and indeed for the world as a whole.* At least for the purposes of this book, particular ideologies can be thus defined as systems of beliefs which purport to offer an account of the sort described in these italicised terms and thereby to furnish us with all that we need to know about how to live and to live well.

In this neutral sense, "ideology" is often synonymous with "creed," "world-view" or "philosophy" as this word occurs in colloquial usages like "What is her philosophy?" Examples of ideologies, thus understood, would include the great monotheistic religions such as Christianity, as well as Freudian psychoanalytic theory and Marxism itself. This can be represented diagrammatically as follows:

	CHRISTIANITY	FREUDIANISM	MARXISM
Account of human condition as is	SIN (etc)	NEUROSIS (etc)	ALIENATION (etc)
Account of the best that can be made of this condition	HEAVEN	FULL GENITALITY	CLASSLESS SOCIETY
Account of what must be done to attain this best condition	REPENT	REMEMBER	REVOLT

This diagram is intended only to illustrate the essential structure of ideological systems and to facilitate discrimination between the kinds of claims which ideologies make. It also brings out the fact that although this book is primarily about political ideology, this is not the only kind of ideological system. Indeed political ideology, to be complete, typically requires assimilation into some more comprehensive world-view, whether sacred or secular. It should be noted, however, that although Christianity, Freudianism and Marxism are all utopian creeds, despite the deep vein of pessimism to be found in each of them, ideology in the neutral sense need not be, and especially with respect to politics very often is not, utopian . It requires only an account of how we can make the best of life, not necessarily how we can generate perfection.

This sense of ideology as "view of life" is appropriately called "neutral", because to describe a belief or an assertion as "ideological" in this sense is not to cast aspersions on either its truth or its moral acceptability. It is merely to locate it within a particular sphere of human interest, namely that of individual and collective conduct as this is informed by ideals and the grounds which are adduced in their support. Ideological claims in this sense are to be distinguished from historical and scientific claims, which are at bottom empirical, as also from those of formal disciplines like mathematics and logic. Ideological claims, on this understanding, are primarily "normative" in their function; that is, they concern the norms which ought to regulate action. They do, however, inevitably rely to a large extent for their justification on empirical claims about the way the world in fact is, as we can come to know it through our experience, as well as on analytical claims about the meanings of terms and concepts and of the logical relationships which can or do hold between them.

This neutral sense of "ideology" and its cognates contrasts with the second kind of usage which I wish to identify, whose distinctive characteristic is that it is always pejorative and negative. This disparaging way of talking about ideology appears to have originated with Napoleon who famously thought that "Cannon killed feudalism. Ink will kill modern society." His hostility towards ideology was essentially that of the practical man of action, who regards abstract theorising as politically ineffectual and a more or less insidious waste of time. A much more sophisticated scepticism about ideology is articulated in the political theorising of Michael Oakeshott.

Oakeshott's hostility to ideology, which is usually associated with his conservative sympathies, is closely related to his hostility to a particular kind of rationalism, namely the sort which informed the approach to politics of the thinkers of the Enlightenment, who believed that past miseries were the product of secular authoritarianism and religious superstition. These thinkers, including de Tracy, consequently believed that the application of reason and scientific method to social problems would yield effective policy prescriptions; and this, according to Oakeshott, has been the dominant opinion in the West ever since. But it is mistaken, so Oakeshott claims, because all that those who thought that they were applying "pure" reason to the social and political problems of their times were in fact able to achieve was an "abridgement" of previous traditions. Thus, very notably, the American Declaration of Independence was no more, and also no less, than an abridgement of, or ideological shorthand for the common law rights of Englishmen as these had been inherited from the Romans and the Normans. To accord such a document, and indeed many works of political theory, quasi-sacred or canonical status was to turn them into mere ideology. Rationalist, ideological politics in Oakeshott's sense of these terms, unanchored in the rich familiarity with concrete political experience which a proper study of history affords, leads to a doomed utopianism in political practice: to a politics whose activists are bent on compelling us, as he puts it to dream other people's dreams, which is intolerable. (Oakeshott: 1962:195-6.)

On this kind of conservative understanding, to describe beliefs as "ideological" is to disparage them for being superficial, crude, impracticable and liable to be drafted into the service of tyrants. Unsurprisingly, there is overlap between this pejorative use of "ideology" associated with conservatism and the radical critique of ideology developed by Karl Marx which has led to the pejorative sense given to the word "ideology" by his followers. In particular, for Marxists, as for conservatives, ideological beliefs are to be fought against because they are barriers to effective political practice and because they shore up systems of oppression.

Marx's critique of ideology, however, is more far-reaching than the conservative one especially in its insistence that ideological beliefs are downright false even though they are not typically insincere. They are rationalisations of self-interest as determined by the social class to which their adherents belong. As such they are products of what Marxists call "false consciousness." Ideological utterances such as declarations of universal human rights are not merely inadequate and misleading: they are pernicious myths which disguise the true nature of class conflict and lend a spurious legitimacy to the exploitation of the many by the few.

We shall consider the Marxist account of ideology further when we come to discuss the Marxist critique of Capitalism. For the moment what needs to be noticed is that we can quite comfortably treat Marxism as itself an ideology, despite Marx's own usage of the term, provided we recognise that when we do so, we are using ideology in the neutral sense and not one which is already freighted with pejorative meaning. It is, of course, then open to us to consider whether Marxism, as an ideology in the neutral sense, is itself vulnerable to either the conservative or the radical critique of ideological discourse and political practice.

We are now in a position to return to the end-of-ideology and the end-of-History theses as these relate to the theory and practice of Communism. According to both theses, communism as an ideology is bankrupt and the world is now embarked upon an inexorable progress towards consensus about ideology in the neutral sense and the elimination from politics of ideology in the negative sense.

If this is right, so it is alleged, we will no longer be compelled to live in an era of potentially cataclysmic conflict between two Super-Powers and their satellites, fuelled by profound and irreconcilable differences of principle about how people should live and how their societies should be organised. Instead, we shall from now on be living in a world which is progressing inexorably towards unanimity in its acceptance of Western values and Western institutions. According to this view, the previously Communist world has unambiguously rejected its hitherto dominant ideology and now wishes to run its societies according to the principles of Capitalism and Democracy. The rest of the world may be expected to follow suit as it is already beginning to do and as it will be increasingly pressured into doing by the rich and powerful countries of the West itself.

For this account to be plausible it is important to stress that the fundamental and irreversible change of heart and mind amongst the peoples of Eastern and Central Europe has not occurred in response to military defeat, forced (or bribed) conversion, or the vagaries of political fashion. It has been the consequence of Communists trying Communism and finding it wanting. Far from beginning to fulfil the utopian promises of Marxism, Communism in practice has led to severe and widespread poverty and to a ruthlessly cruel and totalitarian tyranny. Consequently, and contrary to what some Western Marxists have at first wished to believe, the former inhabitants of Communist regimes, at least initially, did not want to live under a "true," "purified" or "reformed" communist or even socialist regime, albeit one purged of the evils and distortions which characterised the Soviet version of the doctrine. What they wanted was freedom and what they understand by "freedom" was constituted by the entrenched political and economic freedoms of the West:

the rights of individuals to think, speak and live as seems best to themselves rather than to their rulers; their right to accumulate private property and to buy and sell goods and services in free markets; their right to vote in fair elections; their right not to be arrested, incarcerated or killed without due legal process etc..

On this view, (that is the "End-of-Ideology" and/or the "End-of-History" view) Communism was a doctrine which was tried and which failed and whose failure had appalling human consequences. Consequently, experience has shown Communism to be both false and vicious; its defeat has been total and its demise final, just as were the defeat and demise of Fascism in 1945. At the same time, we have witnessed the triumph of liberal democracy as the dominant ideology of the West, not in the sense that the West proved materially and militarily more powerful than its Communist opponents (though it did), but rather in the sense that Communism as a system of beliefs has been exposed as bankrupt.

This is the TOLD thesis and how we evaluate it will depend on how we assess the prospects for democracy, liberalism, socialism and other ideologies considered in the rest of this book. Before concluding this chapter, however it is necessary to try to explicate further the nature and meaning of the claims that History and ideology might now have come to an end. From a common-sense point of view, after all, these claims are absurd. However momentous the fall of Communism may be, it is not going to lead to a world in which events of the sort which historians study will cease to occur. Nor will people now stop having profound and passionate convictions about how political affairs ought to be conducted. It should, therefore, be said at once that neither the end-of-History thesis nor the end-of-ideology thesis includes any such claim. It may also be helpful to point out that we are all familiar with ideological positions which have decisively collapsed: that which justified slavery would be one clear example, as would be that which prescribed the burning of witches or the hanging of children. This is not to say that these practices and the arguments used to justify them are wholly extinct — alas, they are not. Their proponents are rather in the same condition as those who deny that the world is round: they are moral Flat-Earthers.

In trying to make clear what is meant when students of politics, who, like Fukuyama, have been influenced by Hegel, talk about the "end of History" it is well to begin by explaining why History here needs a capital letter. It is for more or less the same reason that God needs one, viz. that we are dealing with something very like the proper name of a person and one who, as the ultimate author of everything that happens, both needs distinctive identification and deserves at least respect if not actual reverence.

Thus History and especially "World-History," for Hegel, as for the great monotheistic religions, constitutes a process in which the purposes of a benign and wholly rational will are progressively revealed and realised. Consequently, individual historical events are to be interpreted and assessed in terms of how they fit into History's master-plan, of which they are more or less significant details. And when the totality of that plan is fully and finally revealed, then History may be said to have come to an end. More accurately if less dramatically, the end of History may be said to be in sight.

The end-of-History thesis, therefore, does not mean that, for Fukuyama, with the collapse of Soviet Communism or, for Hegel, with the triumph of the corporatist Nation State, we have entered an era in which there will no longer be anything for future historians to write about. History as the occurring of interesting events has not come to an end, nor have social change and development. What has allegedly come to an end is History as the progress of human beings towards an understanding of how to live the best possible kind of life, and so of what is the best possible form of social and political arrangement. There is no doubt a temporal gap between the achievement of this understanding and its translation into universal practice, but once the destination of History has been identified, together with the true path which leads to it, then the only thing left for the human race to do is to continue with its inexorable progress along this route and towards this end.

Thus the claim that in the fall of Communism we are encountering "the end of History" is to be understood more in terms of the final and irreversible resolution of an ideological conflict whose outcome had previously seemed uncertain: it is the denouement of the real-life drama which constitutes the history of the world. As a consequence we are now able to understand the true nature and significance of history as History and, having understood it, to accept it. No doubt battles remain to be fought but the outcome of the war is not in doubt.

A possibly useful analogy for understanding why people should want to speak about the end of History as a way of articulating what they see as important truths about the modern world is provided by the theory of evolution. It is clearly not true, in one sense, that the evolutionary process has come to an end. Indeed more new species of beast evolve every year than become extinct (a fact which conservationists are too prone to overlook.) On the other hand, it does make sense also to claim, as Darwin himself seems to have believed, that with the emergence of Man evolution has reached its apogee. Note here, incidentally, that this claim need not be made triumphally: one may well believe, as many have believed, that from a moral point of view evolution, in culminating in Man, has produced a species which is not at all admirable. The same is true of some versions of the end-of-History thesis, in which the condition, convictions and commitments of modern Man (Nietzsche's "Last Man" and Marcuse's "One-Dimensional Man") are held to be deplorable and despicable.

The principal difference between the end-of-History thesis in its Hegelian and neo-Hegelian versions and the end-of-ideology thesis as it was developed in America in the 1950's by Daniel Bell and others, is that the latter was emphatically secular and unmysterious. It was also somewhat parochial, in that it focussed overwhelmingly on the circumstances of the Western world and most notably of America itself. Roughly, what this thesis asserted was that the politics of the New Deal and the Welfare State had, in practice if not in rhetoric, been adopted by all parties in Western countries. Consequently, the politics of passionate and utopian idealism had been exhausted and had given way to a politics of bargaining and compromise within the universally accepted framework of a representative democracy, a mixed economy and a liberal political morality. Fukuyama's end-of-History thesis claims that this is what has started to happen, and will continue happening, in the wake of the collapse of Soviet Communism.

The end-of-ideology thesis was vigorously criticised by Alasdair MacIntyre on the grounds that, first, it confused the decline of Marxism in the West with the decline of ideology as such; and second, that it was itself articulating an unconscious and complacently conservative ideology which gravely misconstrued the moral and political realities of modern industrialised societies. (MacIntyre: 1971: Ch.1.) Fukuyama's end of-History thesis has been criticised with similar vigour by Alan Ryan in the *New York Review of Books,* partly on the grounds that it contradicts itself, partly because it is grounded in a misreading of Hegel, by representing him as a liberal rather than a corporatist, partly because it is ambivalent about the facts of the contemporary world (is Japan or Singapore a democracy, for example?) and perhaps mainly because it is expressive of and/or conducive to a wholly inappropriate ideological smugness, especially amongst Western conservatives. *(New York Review of Books,* March 26, 1992.)

We need not be here detained by the detailed question of whether these criticisms are decisive against particular versions of the claim that ideological conflict is now over and ideological debate therefore a waste of time. What we should note is that it is a very natural interpretation of the anti Communist revolutions in the former Soviet world, which sees them as heralding the end of ideological strife and indicating that Western-style liberal democracy and capitalism will now become the dominant ideology in the East as well as the West. The end-of-ideology and end-of-History theses however, require more than this limited empirical prediction. They require a philosophical formulation which points to what would have to be the case in order for a thesis about the inevitable and universal triumph of democratic liberalism to be true. Such a formulation would assert two propositions: first, that human beings are progressing inexorably towards full rationality; second, that democratic liberalism, when articulated clearly and completely and set against all the relevant facts cannot be rationally rejected by human beings either in theory or in practice.

CHAPTER THREE

DEMOCRACY AND DEMOCRATISM

It seems very difficult to deny at least one part of the thesis that, with the collapse of Communism, democratic liberalism has now finally triumphed over its most serious rival. That is the democratic part. Democracy and democratism have undoubtedly triumphed in the sense that there is now near-universal agreement that democracy is the best form of government and something called "the democratic way of life" is highly desirable.

The ideological triumph of democracy over autocracy and oligarchy took place after the Second World War in the wake of the defeat of Fascism. Thus, in 1949, a UNESCO survey found that: "For the first time in the history of the world no doctrines are advanced as anti-democratic. Practical politicians and political theorists agree in stressing the democratic element in the institutions they defend and the theories they advocate". Similarly, in 1965 the Canadian political theorist, C. B. Macpherson, wrote: "Democracy used to be a bad word. Everybody who was anybody knew that democracy in its original sense of rule by the people or government in accordance with the wishes of the bulk of the people, would be a bad thing — fatal to individual freedom and all the graces of civilised living. That was the position taken by nearly all men of intelligence down to about a hundred years ago. Then within fifty years, democracy became a good thing".

Macpherson went on to distinguish three types of democracy: the "liberal," which is characteristic of the industrialised West; the "economic," which he thought to be what then prevailed in the Communist world; and the "popular" or populist which he claimed was the system adopted by the newly independent countries of the Third World. The latter two types, however, share a commitment to the "one-party state", but this should not, in Macpherson's view, disqualify them from consideration as genuine democracies. (Macpherson: 1965:1.)

It would be naive to accept all this apparent agreement at face value. At most, the post-war consensus about the desirability of democracy constituted an instance of the hypocrisy which La Rochefoucauld described as the tribute which vice pays to virtue. Rulers needed to pretend to be democratic even when they were not, because to be openly against democracy had become taboo after the defeat of Fascism, which took pride in its vigorous and contemptuous anti-democratism. But the realities of oligarchy or minority rule and of autocracy or dictatorship do not melt away because they have been rechristened "democratic." The immediate question, therefore, is whether the collapse of Communism has led to the collapse of all but Western interpretations of democratic ideology and practice.

It is now clear that, in the eyes of the majority of the people who were subjects of the disintegrated Communist regimes, the system under which they lived was emphatically not democratic in any sense, including the economic one. The same is true of at least many of the "populist" democracies in Africa, Asia and Latin America, where there is widespread rejection of "one-party democracy" in favour of multi-party democracy — a trend which is receiving substantial support from the World Bank and allied organisations dominated by Western Capitalism. There does seem to be reason to think, therefore, that not only has democracy, variously and vaguely defined, come to be the only internationally respectable form of domestic government: specifically Western-style, multi-party and "liberal" democracy, seems to have triumphed over its competitors in the ideological struggle to be recognised as the best or only true form of democracy.

Does this mean that Western-style, multi-party democracy has now been shown to be the ideal form of political organisation such that all reasonable people can, in the not-too-long run, be expected to recognise it as such in political deed as well as political word? If so, it would follow that, at least as far as the liberal understanding of democracy is concerned, the end-of-ideology/end-of-

History theses are confirmed, because to dispute the superiority of Western democracy over its rivals would now be as irrational as denying the roundness of the earth or the wickedness of slavery.

There are three main reasons for thinking that this may not be so. The first is conceptual and has to do with whether there is indeed consensus about what we mean by Western democracy. The second relates to questions of empirical fact and points most notably to China and the Middle East as reasons for thinking that Western democracy is very far from having triumphed decisively over all possible rivals. The third concerns the values which are thought to be uniquely protected and promoted by Western democracy. It questions whether the arguments for democracy are really so cogent that they are bound to prevail wherever people are or become rational enough to understand them clearly and to feel their full force.

The conceptual dispute focuses on the fact that even within Western democracies there is vigorous dispute amongst democrats about what democracy really is and what in practice it entails. There are two main schools of thought: that of the defenders of "representative" democracy and that of the advocates of "participatory" democracy. The former see democracy as a matter of the people's electing representatives to make decisions about how they shall be governed. The latter complain that this is quite inadequate as a means for ensuring that people have power over the political decisions which will vitally affect them and argue that there will only be true democracy when people can actually participate in the making of those decisions. This complaint was articulated with characteristic vim by Rousseau who wrote: "Sovereignty cannot be represented ... Unless the people in person ratifies a law, it is not a law. The English people thinks itself free, but it is badly mistaken. It is free only during a general parliamentary election: as soon as a parliament has been elected the people is again enslaved, it is nothing. The use which this people makes of the brief moment of its liberty shows that it deserves to lose it." (Rousseau:1761:1915:94.)

This dispute, however, can be resolved by paying careful attention to what democracy means and how it works. It then becomes possible to rebut Rousseau's charge and to show that, while more active participation in decision-making by ordinary people may be desirable, it also may not be, and certainly such participation is not a necessary condition for the practice of genuine and full-blooded democracy.

To see why this apparently paradoxical claim should be true we need to examine what precisely is involved in the exercise of political power. Now, the essential feature of democratic government and politics is revealed in the etymology of the word "democracy." Literally, democracy means that the people have power, which here means that ultimate political power resides with all the people equally. Democracy is popular sovereignty, as opposed to oligarchy[1], (where ultimate power or sovereignty is in the hands of an elite few) and to autocracy (where all power is in the hands of an individual).

This is important because it suggests that democracy is not necessarily one of the things that it is often mistaken for (for example by Macpherson as quoted above) — namely "majority rule". Majorities do not rule in representative democracies in the sense of making, administering or enforcing the rules under which the citizens of a particular society must live. Noticing this, critics of representative democracy have argued that the countries which claim to subscribe to this ideal are not really democracies at all because the people do not rule in them, although they both can and should and, indeed, would if "representative" democracies were to become properly "participatory" ones.

It is no doubt technologically possible to devise means whereby every adult (and, for that matter, not so adult) member of society could participate in ruling by listening to debates about proposed legislation on radio, contributing to them and casting a vote at

1. Etymologically, "aristocracy" is a better word than oligarchy here, because whereas "oligarchy" means that a few rule (and only a few actually ever rule in modern democracies) aristocracy means that ultimate power or sovereignty resides with the class of the best people. I avoid "aristocracy" because it suggests to the modern ear that "the best" are being defined in terms of hereditary social rank. Later I shall sometimes speak of meritocracy. The ideal word would be oligocracy.

the end of them. In effect this would be democratic government in which all legislation had to be passed by referendum. This would be formidably complex and time-consuming; it would probably be extremely inefficient and might well be widely unpopular as well, since most people think they have better things to do with their lives than to be constantly participating in political discussion and decision-making.

What is undeniable is that, under such a system, the majority would come much nearer to ruling than they presently do in Western democracies. Less drastic methods for giving people more direct control over the decisions which affect them depend on devolving those decisions to smaller units, such as local government institutions and the work-place. Even here, however, there would be considerable constraints on the amount of real autonomy that could be achieved given the high degree of interdependence which characterises large modern societies. Factories cannot take decisions independently of the industry in which they work, which in turn operates within the constraints of the wider economy. Nor can local government enjoy autonomy beyond what it can finance on its own and this is unlikely, for example, to include its defence and security needs.

In the same way if states were very much smaller, so that they served "face-to-face" rather than preponderantly anonymous societies, they might well purchase the possibility of more direct participation in domestic decision-making at the cost of much greater dependence, in other areas, on states over whose affairs they have no democratic control whatsoever. We shall consider this point further in Chapter 7.

What is crucial here, however, is to notice that democracy does not require that the people actually rule. It only requires that they exercise decisive power over those who do rule. It is a fallacy to think that the greater the amount of majority rulings, the more real democracy there is; or conversely that the fewer the opportunities there are for direct participation in hands-on decision-making, the less we have of real democracy. The fallacy consists in thinking that the only effective political power which people can exercise over their governments is the direct power to make rules. This is not so and only appears to be so as long as we have an unduly restricted notion of what it is to exercise, or simply to have power.

Much power is indeed direct in the manner of its exercise. The highwayman's power, based on the threat "Your money or your life", is of this sort. So is any exercise of power which depends on being able to cause people to do things which they otherwise might not do, by making promises, offering rewards, imposing sanctions and, indeed, by physically manipulating them. Nor are coercion and inducement the only ways in which power can be directly exercised: rational persuasion and appeal to authority are also often effective means of causing people to do things which they otherwise might not have chosen to do. That rulers are heavily dependent on the exercise of this kind of power in a democracy is one of the most striking and attractive features of this form of government.

Power may, however, also be exercised indirectly or passively in the sense that the person exercising power does not need actually to do anything in order to bring about behaviour modification. This occurs when people modify their behaviour so as to conform to what they believe to be the wishes of others whom they, again, believe will react in a certain undesirable way if they do not do so. In the not too distant past, a new teacher might have caused a class of pupils to stand up simply by entering a classroom. Not only need she have issued no command: she may have been wholly unaware of the existence of any rule or custom in the school relating to standing up when teachers enter classrooms; she may even have disliked what she perceived as an unduly formal practice. Nevertheless, it was in virtue of the power she possessed that pupils, who were presumably not otherwise disposed to rise, rose.

This kind of power depends on anticipated reactions and is the kind of power, for example, which, you — hoped-for future readers — are presently exercising over me in relation to what I am writing and indeed to the fact that I am writing at all. The power of anticipated reactions is particularly important for an understanding of what democracy is, or can be, and how it works in its representative form, in which the majority of the people do not rule but rather elect rulers at periodic intervals. This is

23

because rulers so elected are constantly concerned, and not only at election time, to conform their behaviour to what they think will please the electorate sufficiently to secure their re-election. Conversely, their opponents will be constantly seeking to expose those in power as unworthy of re-election and to present themselves as more desirable future office-holders from the point of view of the voters. In short, in representative, Western democracies ultimate power resides with the people because democratic institutions ensure that the conduct of politicians is continuously controlled by public opinion.

The nature of these institutions is determined by what is logically, or causally necessary to ensure that this control by public opinion is effective. Thus, any system of government which is intended to compel rulers to conform their conduct to the wishes of at least a majority of those who are ruled must have some form of voting procedure which enables the ruled to express their wishes. Minimally, in a democracy where much of the people's power is reactional, i.e. based on anticipated reactions, this will require free, fair and (too often overlooked) frequent elections. "Free" typically focuses on absence of intimidation and bribery and secrecy of balloting. "Fair", typically means that all can vote and all votes count equally. "Frequent," in practice, means that terms of office are set, at least for national leaders, at between four and seven years, this being thought of as neither too short to enable government to be effective, nor too long to ensure that government is responsive.

For such elections to be effective in giving expression to the voters' preferences, there must be ready access to relevant information and argument; and this means freedom of expression. Above all, if rulers are to be constantly, and not just periodically, concerned to satisfy their constituents there must be a real prospect that they will be replaced by their opponents. That requirement means that there must be freedom of opposition or genuinely competitive politics. For this reason the best test of how democratic a society is, is to ask the questions: "What happens to those who seek to replace the government by winning elections?" and "How realistic are the prospects that such opponents may succeed?" It is because one-party states, whether Communist or populist, have little or no tolerance of opposition that they do not and cannot pass this test.

Where the machinery for effective opposition to the government is in place and working, the people will exercise full democratic control over their political circumstances. This is not, of course, to deny that in practice the institutions of Western, representative democracies are in many ways inadequate or defective in this respect. Opponents may be secretly silenced by bribery, black-mail or worse. Office-holders may, and often do, abuse their power, on the pretext of serving the public interest, in order to further their personal political interests. Plutocrats may manipu-late access to information, and cultural and educational calami-ties may breed citizens who are cynical, apathetic and ignorant about democracy. Poverty may both reinforce and be reinforced by a sense of political impotence. But these flaws, huge as they are, need to be remedied: they do not demonstrate that the whole system, based on reactional power, is inherently fraudulent and needs to be abandoned.

Participationists are also right that there may be very good rea-sons for wanting people to be more directly involved in the deci-sions which affect their lives through the communities in which they live. Such participation may promote a sense of civic duty, or strengthen sentiments of affection for, and loyalty towards the community as a whole. It may have psychological spin-offs in terms of enhancing confidence and self-respect, or educational ones in terms of developing the capacity for rational argument. However, the desirability of all these things does mean, (just as the possibility of securing them through more direct participation in political decision-making does not mean,) that representative democracy is a failure as a means of ensuring that ultimate politi-cal power resides with all the people equally, as democracy requires.

For these reasons, I think we can reject the claim that Western democracy has not triumphed in the wake of the collapse of Communism because Western democracy has not got its own theoretical act together. But what of the empirical claim that Western democracy has not in fact triumphed in practice, as Fukuyama and others would have us believe?

The clearest exceptions to the general democratising trend in world politics are to be found in the Middle East, especially the Islamic states, and the far East, in particular China. Here autocracy on the one hand, and Communist oligarchy on the other, appear to be firmly entrenched in the hands of rulers who are prepared to use extreme force to crush any potential opposition. This was made gruesomely clear in Tiananmen Square on June 3 and 4, 1989. Similarly in the 1991 war against Iraq, to the horror of the Kurds and the Shi-ites, the American leadership proved incapable of overthrowing Saddam Hussein, whose ruthlessly brutal dictatorship they had previously been comparing to Hitler's.

Nevertheless, the counter-examples of China and the Arab world are far from decisive against the democratic component in end-of-ideology, triumph-of-liberal-democracy accounts of how we should interpret the fall of Soviet Communism. For it might seem that what most obviously led to the collapse of Russia was economic failure. If so, there is good reason to think similar economic forces will eventually be decisive in undermining Chinese communism: indeed, there is quite a lot of evidence that China is already, in practice, renouncing the more sclerotic features of the centrally planned economy in favour of freeing up markets, endorsing private enterprises and initiatives, and seeking to unleash individual industry and ingenuity.

If one adds to this alleged economic imperative, the claim that free markets in industrialising societies themselves generate an ultimately irresistible demand for political equality, then it is easy to see why people might expect China's present persistence as a Communist oligarchy to be a temporary phenomenon.

Similarly with the Sheikhdoms, monarchies, theocracies and military dictatorships of the Middle East. To be sure, these regimes are not all equally "bad" from the point of view of liberal-democratic values. But none of them could be described as democracies in any sense which could be recognised by Western democrats. To say this, it should be emphasised, is not to pass hostile moral judgment on these regimes. For even on the debatable assumption that democracy is indeed the best form of

government, it might still be argued that social, cultural, economic, religious and historical factors all combine, for the time
being at least, to make Western-style democracy wholly inappropriate, either as ideology or as a form of government, in this part
of the world. Nevertheless, it remains open to an optimistic liberal democrat to maintain that these circumstances will change,
indeed that they must change, and that when they do, and liberal
democracy becomes a viable choice for the peoples of these
countries, that is what they will choose.

A more cynical account of the present deviance of the Middle
East from the liberal-democratic norm needs to be mentioned,
not out of schadenfreude, but because it bears on the question of
how durable that deviance is like to prove. On this view, the only
reason why non-democratic and non-liberal rule continues
unchecked and uncondemned in the Middle East is that the West
cannot do without the oil that is located there, while the countries
of the region continue to prosper as a consequence of this
Western dependence.

This has two consequences which make for the stability of the
existing non-democratic regimes. First, the West has no interest
in seeking to change the form of government which prevails in
the countries of the region or, at least, not in a way that would
risk upsetting the stability of oil supplies. Thus, so the cynic
would allege, America used the out-of-action status of Russia to
dragoon the United Nations Security Council into authorising
war on Iraq to protect its oil-rich allies who had been attacked, or
who were threatened with attack, by Saddam. The ideals of liber-
al-democracy, of human rights, or of common humanity had
nothing to do with it, which is why Saddam (at the time of writing) is still in power.

Secondly, the lucrativeness of the oil trade deters the domestic
population from rebelling because they are prospering materially.
We need to remember that Gaddafi and Saddam (before the war),
as well as the more Western-friendly autocrats of the region,
have, on the whole, enjoyed great popularity among their peoples
because they have been able to use oil revenues to effect huge
improvements in the standard of living of their populations. In
combination, these two consequences of the dependence of the

Western world on Arab oil mean that there is neither domestic nor foreign pressure on the rulers of these autocracies to embark on democratic reforms, which would clearly run contrary to their own interests.

If all this is correct, however, it does not necessarily confute the view that Western democracy has won or, at least, is winning the ideological battle for the political allegiance of the whole world. It may, rather, give some further support for the view that it is only a matter of time before this undemocratic part of the world also comes to see the light and to reform itself in a liberal-democratic direction. For if illiberalism and non-democracy are only tolerated in the Middle East because of dependency on oil, then these illiberal, undemocratic regimes are not likely to survive drastic changes in the nature of that dependency. One of two such possible, though diametrically opposite, kinds of change can be plausibly anticipated. First, the dependence may diminish as alternative reliable sources of cheap energy are developed. Secondly, the dependence may persist but the perceived risk that hostile rulers might cut off supplies or intolerably raise the price of oil may grow to the point where the West is no longer prepared to adhere to the principle of non-intervention in the domestic affairs of foreign states. In the case of either of these eventualities being realised, albeit for different reasons, the West might well decide to try to impose liberal democracy by force.

On conceptual and empirical grounds, then, there seem to be no adequate reason for thinking that Western democratism could not become a universally acceptable political doctrine as the end-of-History thesis maintains. It is internally coherent and consonant with present and foreseeable facts. Already it seems to be becoming more and more widely taken for granted that liberal democracy is the best form of government and it is by no means implausible to suggest that this belief may now come to appear everywhere as natural as the belief that people are born with nationalities which determine by whom they should and should not be governed: British should be governed only by British, Indians by Indians, Chinese by Chinese etc..[2]

2. This claim is explored further in the chapter on "Nationalism" below. For the moment we should be warned by the thought that, despite its apparent self-evidence, this claim may be historically very eccentric and philosophically absurd.

However, the triumph-of-liberal-democracy thesis requires more than simply growing acceptance of the view that democracy is the best form of government: if it is to be proof against the vagaries of passing fashion, this belief in democracy needs also to be rationally justifiable. Specifically, it needs to be shown that in the post-Communist era which we are now entering, societies will be better served if they are governed according to the principles and practices of political equality rather than those of political elitism. Despite the Pavlovian tendency to react with a warm glow of approval to the word "equality" and its cognates and with disapproval to "elite" and "elitist," the case for political elitism is, on the face of it, very strong, and that for political equality very unconvincing.

The anti-democratic, anti-egalitarian case has never been put more thoroughly, more vigorously and more persuasively than by Plato in *The Republic*. Later elitists on the Right, such as the seventeenth century Bishop Filmer who advocated the Divine Right of Kings, relied on arguments that could be quite easily rebutted by more liberal thinkers such as John Locke. The advocacy of elitism in Marx's doctrine of the "Dictatorship of the Proletariat", and Lenin's claims about the "Vanguard of the Revolution", led to precisely the combination of tyranny and incompetence which were the ultimate causes of the collapse of Communism. However Plato's arguments for "Philosopher Kings", or a benevolent dictatorship, continue to constitute a formidable challenge to reflective democrats.[3]

The essence of Plato's case is simply stated. The central problem of government is to discover a way of ensuring that those who govern are possessed both of the knowledge and the wisdom necessary in order to secure the public interest, and of sufficient virtue to ensure that they in fact govern in the interest of the public or the community as a whole, rather than in their private or sectional interest. Clearly, if everybody were, by nature, equally

3. A challenge taken up with formidable energy and erudition by Sir Karl Popper in his *The Open Society and its Enemies* (Vol 1.) which has itself been vigorously challenged, for example, by Robin Barrow in *Plato, Utilitarianism and Education.*

capable of being educated in political wisdom and virtue, everybody would be equally capable of ruling. But palpably they are not. Therefore those who have the greatest aptitude for learning the arts of good government should be selected and prepared by an appropriate education eventually to become societies' rulers. This education will ensure that future rulers know whatever it is that they will need to know and also that their character is so formed that they are immune to corruption of any sort. They will be deaf to the siren appeals of money and sex and, far from being liable to an addiction to political power, they will actively dislike it — which is precisely a condition for being trusted with its exercise. Nor will those who lack the requisite knowledge, or who might be tempted to use political power to gratify their baser desires, be able to do so since they will have no access to political power. In this way, says Plato, government will ensure as far as is humanly possible, that everyone lives the best, the most fulfilling and the happiest life of which they are capable.

It is very difficult for a democrat to deny the objections to democracy which Plato and other meritocrats commonly urge. Thus, people are not equal with respect to their aptitude for exercising political power and it is implausible to claim that they can be made so. Moreover, politicians who are dependent on popular support have a strong interest in cultivating the appearance of virtue but little in cultivating the reality, and indeed quite a strong incentive to engage in a high degree of ruthlessness and dishonesty. Undoubtedly, or so it seems, the world would be a happier place if political power were the exclusive preserve of the wise and the good.

Nevertheless, there is a decisive answer to these objections which is based on concrete and practical considerations grounded in historical experience. Thus, benevolent dictatorship is no doubt fine if you can first reliably identify the individuals who are best suited to rule and then ensure that they do not become corrupted in the course of ruling, like Nero and Henry the Eighth, who both started out as benevolent autocrats. Since, however, we can't do this, we will be better off with an egalitarian system which enables us to limit, by evicting them from office, the damage which our rulers can do to us.

The case for multi-party democracy, on this kind of argument, rests on an acceptance of the empirical truth of Lord Acton's much misquoted dictum: "Power tends to corrupt, and absolute power corrupts absolutely." Consequently, what we need above all from our system of government is protection from bad rulers rather than the generation of infallibly good ones, for the latter (Platonic) ideal is unattainable. And in practice history teaches us that under democracy, in comparison with all forms of self-styled meritocracy, there is a greater chance of promoting civil tranquillity, of protecting individual liberties, of securing justice, of generating prosperity and of reducing poverty. Democracy may not be able to guarantee these political goods, nor by itself supply them in an adequate abundance, but all things considered, democratic polities tend to perform better in terms of these goods than undemocratic ones, at least over the long term. The defence of multi-party democracy, which might consequently prove universally acceptable in the wake of the collapse of Communism and of one-party states in the Third World, might be that articulated in Winston Churchill's aphorism: "Party democracy is the worst of all forms of government, except for all the others".

It might be thought that the TOLD thesis, as far as democracy is concerned is now strongly supported. Western democracy turns out to be coherent in a way that "one-party democracy" is not. Economic and other developments internationally seem to favour the spread of democracy and to disfavour the continued survival of oligarchies and autocracies. And in practice democracy seems to protect and promote, better than any other system, what are widely perceived to be universal human rights. However, growing acceptance that democracy is the best form of government is not enough to vindicate the the TOLD thesis as a whole.

If it were, then in the phrase "liberal democracy," the word "liberal" would be doing no work other than to distinguish true and coherent multi-party democracy from the fraudulent and incoherent one-party imposters which style themselves "economic" and "popular" democracy. But when people speak of liberal democracy they are typically referring to more than a set of procedures for transacting political business. What they have in mind is a society which is committed to certain ideals. Adherents of liberal democracy hold that these ideals describe the best kind of life to

31

which human beings can aspire and the only kind of society in which they are able to live this life. Opponents of liberal democracy complain not only that liberal democracy fails to secure the ideals to which it professes itself committed, but also that these ideals are themselves unworthy and neglect what is most profoundly required for true human self-fulfilment. Liberal democratism is thus an ideology in the neutral sense because it offers an account of the nature of the human condition both as it is and as it could and should become. It also proposes a set of practices for transforming our presently flawed and inadequate circumstances so that we may at last embark on the path to true human perfection.

It is, however, for reasons which will become clear, the liberal rather than the democratic component that supplies the moral and ideological core of liberal democratism and it is, therefore, to liberalism that we now turn.

CHAPTER FOUR

LIBERALISM

It is regrettable that in the vocabulary of many supporters of Western democracy, the word "democracy" has come to be used as a shorthand for "liberal democracy". This generates confusion because it suggests that a commitment to liberalism and a commitment to democracy are the same thing. As we shall see the relations between liberalism and democratism are complex and their subtlety needs to be understood if we are to be able to evaluate the compound set of beliefs which constitute "liberal democratism" (or "democratic liberalism"), as a coherent ideology.

Briefly, at the heart of liberalism is a particular understanding of human freedom and at the heart of democratism a particular interpretation and justification of the principle of equality. But both freedom and equality are notoriously tricky concepts which often seem to overlap, sometimes apparently merging into one another and at other times diverging sharply so that they stand in direct contrast to one another. Similarly with the relations between liberalism and democracy. In some contexts liberal principles appear to entail democratic government; in others, democracy poses a severe threat to liberal ideals and institutions; most commonly, perhaps, liberalism in practice favours democracy, and democracy in practice promotes liberalism without its being always, or necessarily the case that this should happen.

In considering how real and enduring the post-Communist triumph of liberal democracy is likely to prove, we need to disentangle liberalism from democracy. In particular, we need to consider the possibilities that liberal values may come to be better served in the future — as arguably they have been on occasion in the past — under non-democratic political arrangements, and that multi-party democracy may come to support non-liberal or anti-liberal political values. One obvious way in which the first of these possibilities might be realised would be if, at a global level, it became clear that a democratic world government would be either unable or unwilling to protect what liberals claim are inalienable individual rights. The second possibility would be realised if democratic institutions led, in a number of societies, to the election of leaders committed to Stalinist or Fascist values or to the enforcement of conformity to the teachings of a particular religion.

In terms of the TOLD thesis, what we now need to consider is not whether democracy, as understood in contemporary Western liberal societies, is the best way of securing liberal values, but whether those values are such that they must increasingly compel the allegiance of a humanity which is assumed to be becoming progressively more rational. Obviously, this requires a clear conception of what "liberal values" are supposed to be.

It is crucial for an understanding of liberalism to realise that it began life, not as a moderate doctrine, still less as a conservative one, but as a profoundly radical reaction against previously received truths. I describe this reaction as "profoundly radical" because it was not merely a matter of the vehement rejection of a previously dominant orthodoxy: it was a rejection of the whole notion of authoritative orthodoxy. As such, liberalism is not only a political thesis; it is a creed which has roots in theology and epistemology as well as in the domain of moral philosophy. It is this that makes liberalism a genuine ideology, with a specific account of what it is to be human, what it is for a human being to live well and what human beings must do if they are to succeed in living well.

A useful way, therefore, to begin thinking about political liberalism is to conceive of it as the youngest sibling of a *prima facie* unlikely union between scepticism and optimism, the older siblings being Protestantism and the empiricism which led to the spectacular emergence of modern science. The sceptical component in liberalism asserts that all authority is to be distrusted: in religion, the authority of the Church; in science, the authority of

Aristotle and other Ancients; in politics, the authority of the absolute monarch. The optimistic component asserts that while you cannot trust authority, you can trust yourself: in religion, your conscience; in science, the evidence of your senses; in politics, your judgment. Crucial to both components is confidence in the power of reason; hence the association of liberalism with "rationalism" understood as the doctrine that one should only believe what there are good reasons for believing, and not accept any claims based on alleged revelation alone, on the authority of supposed and powerful experts, on superstition or intuition or tradition.

The extreme version of rationalism is articulated in Descartes' famous "Method of Doubt" which proposes that we should only believe what it is impossible to doubt. Thus we should doubt the evidence of our senses and even the conclusions of chains of mathematical calculation unless and until we can find some indubitable reason for not doing so. Descartes is, of course, enthusiastic about this procedure, not because it does justice to genuine doubts which he experiences but, on the contrary, because he is wholly confident that he has already found an indubitable basis for trusting in the veridical character of sense experience and the reliability of logical reasoning. This basis is the existence of a benevolent God, who cannot by His nature have created us for a condition of permanent and irremediable error. And the existence of such a God is itself, for Descartes, indubitably and immediately inferable from the fact of our own existence, something which, in the case of ourselves, it is wholly impossible to doubt.[1]

Although Empiricism is usually contrasted with Rationalism in histories of philosophy, this is to emphasise the Empiricists' claim that the basis of all knowledge is experience, and that we cannot reach true conclusions by the unaided application of

1. This is Descartes' famous "*Cogito ergo sum*" argument, which, in French, is "*Je pense, donc, je suis.*" In English the translation is invariably "I think, therefore I am,". But "*penser*" is often, in seventeenth century usage, better rendered as "to be conscious" and it is certainly the whole phenomenon of consciousness, rather than the activity of cerebration alone which Descartes makes definitive of what it is to exist as a person and which he thinks allows us to deduce the existence of God.

speculative reasoning to particular questions in advance of garnering whatever evidence experience may provide. However, in the sense given above, empiricism is itself a species of rationalism, which is equally hostile to brute authority, fantastical superstition and uncritically accepted tradition as a basis for attaining truth. It is, therefore, not surprising that, in practice, liberal political theory has been very closely associated with an empiricist theory of knowledge, an association reinforced by the ascription of fatherhood, in both cases, to the seventeenth century English philosopher, John Locke.

The fundamental tenet of Locke's political theory is that the allocation and exercise of political power must be based only on principles which can be discovered and defended by human reason, which is taken to be a distinctive and universal faculty possessed by all sane adults. This might be thought to be truistic and trivial. After all, human reason can supply arguments for virtually every conceivable political arrangement, including all the illiberal ones, and the most radically various political systems have in fact been argued for on the basis of what their proponents took to be universally cogent reasons. What other basis for argument could there be?

The liberal understanding of human reason, however, is distinctive, and what makes it distinctive is of decisive importance for the substance of liberal political doctrine. Two features of this understanding are critical.

First, reason is understood by liberals to be the faculty which human beings employ in deciding how to act. They find themselves in situations where they have a choice between different courses of action and, in the light of their short-term and long-term desires, they select the one which seems best suited to the securing of their ends. This is an instrumental understanding of reason which is sometimes mistaken for the whole of reasoning. It evaluates different courses of action as means to given ends, the ends being given by our desires. However, if this were the whole picture it would be intolerable from the point of view of human freedom, for it would suggest the truth of the thesis of determinism, i.e. the thesis that human beings have no free will, and this is a doctrine which no liberal can coherently accept and which, as we shall see, is in any case either incoherent or demonstrably false.

The illusion of determinism arises from a splitting of the faculty of reasoning from the faculty of desiring. Thus, as in the instrumental account given above, we can employ our reason to select between means to our ends, but the ends themselves, so the determinist alleges, are given by our desires, which in turn are thought of as the product of factors or forces over which we have no ultimate control. For example, I want to obtain a bicycle. Reason tells me that I can satisfy this want by stealing one or by buying one. If I am to buy one, I must either use money I already have, in which case I won't be able to use that money for other purposes, or I must acquire more. If the latter I can steal it or earn it, or sell something to raise it, and so on. There are a whole series of different things I can do in order to get myself a bicycle. Which one I choose depends on my judgment about the relative efficiency of different courses of action in satisfying my desire in a way which is optimally consonant with other desires I have, (like not wishing to go to gaol, or to sell my wedding ring). I may even reflect on what it is I want the bicycle for: for convenience, say, or status or as an investment. This in turn may prompt me to think about whether obtaining a bicycle is the best way of satisfying these longer-term desires. But even if it does, it will still be the desires that I happen to have which determine what I do, and over them I have no control.

Crucial to this initially plausible, but repugnant argument is a picture of desires as quasi-physical forces — urges, revulsions, motives, etc. — which we just have inside us and which exert a certain pressure in a certain direction, such that, whichever combination of desires turns out to be the strongest will impel us, willy-nilly, to behave in one way rather than another. This picture has encouraged people, especially those impressed by pre-quantum mechanics, to think that human behaviour can be explained causally by searching out the origins of these forces called "desires." Typically these origins are found in our genetic inheritance interacting with critical features of the family and the society in which we were born and raised.

If our "choices" are determined by our desires and our desires by things that are "given" to us by nature and nurture, there is clearly no room for genuinely free choice. When to this proposition is added the claim that the desires people have do not always, or usually, correspond with what is in their real interests to desire, then the foundation is laid for a politics which is indifferent to the claim that people should be treated as autonomous agents (for they are not) and that government should take account of what they believe themselves to want, (for that may well not be what they really need.) The thesis of determinism is therefore potentially ruinous to both liberalism and democratism. It is also ruinous (though determinists usually deny this,) to the whole project of morality, understood as including the attempt to make right choices and to commend the adoption of some courses of action and to condemn others. Since people cannot help what they do because they do not really choose it, praising and blaming them for their behaviour is irrational and trying to conform our own conduct to what we take to be right is futile.

However, the account of desires which I have suggested undergirds all forms of determinism, is mistaken, and when we see why, we shall also understand what human freedom of action really consists in and how it relates to human rationality. This in turn will supply us with the metaphysical basis for the account of individual freedom which is at the heart of the liberal understanding of political freedom.

Consider, in contrast to the case of the person wanting a bicycle, the case of someone who wakes up, perhaps suffering somewhat from the effects of over-indulgence, and wonders whether to get up and go to work or to call in sick and stay in bed. Such a person obviously has a desire to adopt the latter course. Almost certainly there will also be desires, though less immediate ones, which the person wishes to satisfy and which require going to work — not getting fired, for example, or not suffering a guilty conscience. Now at least at the time when the decision is being made, these desires are given. The person cannot help wanting what they want at this particular moment any more than they can help feeling mildly sick. But that doesn't mean that these desires are immutable, or that the person's conduct will be determined by the relative strength of these desires, regardless of what the agent might try to do to thwart them. On the contrary, in this situation, it is clear that the one thing the agent cannot do is to say: "Well, since I am a determinist I will just lie here and wait to see which of the competing forces, all of which are outside my control, wins the day and whether my desire to stay at home proves strong enough to bind me beneath the sheets, or whether my anxieties turn out to be powerful enough to eject me from bed."

This cannot be done, not because we are all prisoners of an unshakeable illusion that we have free choice, but because the project of waiting to see what will happen in a case like this is incoherent: we cannot conceive of what might be meant by trying to carry it out. Indeed it can only be made sense of as the rationalisation of a decision to stay in bed without the inconvenience of believing oneself responsible for that decision. (This is what Sartre and other Existentialists have in mind when they speak of "bad faith.")

Instead, what happens in a case such as this one, is that people confronted with a choice think about the pros and cons of different possible courses of action and then "make up their minds" about what to do. In the process of these deliberations they decide what they most want. Desires are thus not fixed but fluid and amenable to being changed by rational reflection; and it is just this capacity to mould our behaviour to what reason prescribes that constitutes freedom of choice and action or, more archaically, free will. This does not mean that some behaviour is not free, and clearly people do often act out of internal as well as external compulsions which have sources outside themselves. They also are often unaware of the forces, psychological and social, which are acting upon them, with the consequence that they either misconstrue their own motives, or are unable to conform their behaviour to what they consciously believe to be the best thing to do. Nor need a libertarian — that is, someone who believes that human beings really do possess free will, such that people can act otherwise than they do — deny that all our choices are circumscribed within a range of possibilities. There is a limit to the scope of our freedom. The laws of nature in particular set limits to what people can choose to do.

What metaphysical libertarians must deny, as must political

liberals, is that all our behaviour is always and only the product of forces over which we have no control, whether we are aware of them or not. Normally, indeed, our behaviour is not so determined, but is rather the product of our unforced assent. Thus, it is true that by taking thought we cannot add one cubit to our stature, but it does not follow, and is in fact false, that we can never change anything about our lives by taking thought.

Although this is somewhat under-emphasised in the vast literature on the subject, the denial of determinism in all its forms, especially perhaps "historical" determinism, is logically fundamental to any coherent account of liberalism. Put positively, you cannot consistently be a liberal without also being a libertarian. This is because the liberal account of political freedom is based on the belief that human beings are capable of acting freely and rationally, that normally they do act in this way, and that to the extent that they don't they should be encouraged to do so. This belief is what should determine their moral conduct towards one another and the political constitution and behaviour of their government. Above all, at the heart of liberal politics is the prescription: "Respect the autonomy of every individual."

At this point the notion of freedom in liberalism enters into necessary relations with the notion of equality. For if the capacity to act rationally, intelligently, freely and morally is taken to be something which all human beings have in common, and is the central fact about them in virtue of which they are persons, then this will also be the fundamental fact which must be taken into account when considering how they should treat and be treated by one another. However, if every individual is a rational autonomous agent and ought to be treated as such, then everyone ought to be treated equally in this respect. This doesn't mean that all people are assumed to be equally good at reasoning; simply that everyone has the capacity to think about what they want to do and to be, and to act accordingly. In this sense everyone ought to be treated equally because they are equally free, that is, they are equally possessed of, if not equally adept in, the use of reason.

Now, it is a legitimate, if initially puzzling question why people should be treated in accordance with what in fact they are; why, for example they should be treated as rational, free and equal in the relevant, liberal, senses simply because that is what they are. This difficult question can only be noted here.[2] Meanwhile we must acknowledge that the TOLD thesis certainly requires that, as people grow in understanding of what it is they need in order to live well in relation to one another, they will come to accept the liberal principles of freedom and equality as being what rationality prescribes. What we now, therefore, need to address is what in practice it would mean to treat everyone equally as a free, moral agent. We need to be clear, that is, about what both champions and critics of liberal democracy mean by liberty and equality, so that we can see what kind of society is supposed to be perfecting itself as liberal democracy triumphs world-wide in the aftermath of Communism.

The most fundamental sense in which for liberals "all men (and women) are equal" is originally, though no longer peculiarly, Christian: everyone is equal because everyone is equally and uniquely precious to God. There is no chosen race or caste or class for the early Christians. Slaves are the equals of their masters, women of men, Gentiles of Jews etc.. Each of us possesses an immortal soul about whose present and ultimate well-being God cares as much as it is possible to care. In short, we are equal because we are equally sacred.

This conception of equality retains much of its power and appeal in secularised form as the doctrine of (fundamental and inalienable) natural or human rights. There are certain things which may not be done to anyone and other things that must be done to everyone simply because they are human-beings. In a justly

---

2. The general problem is the one made famous by Hume, which usually goes under the name "The Naturalist Fallacy." The fallacy is supposed to consist in thinking you can ever validly derive a statement about what ought to be the case from any set of statements about what is the case. Bare facts do not of themselves supply compelling reasons for action. I think the general answer is that if we know the kind of life which will most deeply satisfy a person's nature, we can infer that she ought to do those things which will enable her to live such a life. General ethical doctrines can similarly be inferred from facts about human nature in general (if there is such a thing.)

influential modern version of this doctrine, Ronald Dworkin claims that reason requires us to treat people with "equality of concern and respect."

Quite how this doctrine cashes out politically in either its Christian or secular forms is hotly contested, especially in respect of the provision of goods and services by taxing some to supply what others lack. This will be discussed in connection with socialism. It is also unclear what, in practice, treating other people equally as unique centres of consciousness and freedom involves at the level of either interpersonal relationships or of political organisation — in particular whether this needs to be democratic, or in some other way based on consent. There are, however, at least two political implications of this account of what persons most fundamentally are which seem relatively clear. These relate to what is usually known as the "equal liberty principle"; and to equality before the law.

The case for equal liberty has never been put more forcefully or more elegantly than by Thomas Hobbes, (though it has been made by many others as well) whose argument, much simplified and paraphrased, goes as follows. The human condition is such that, in seeking the satisfaction of their manifold and various desires, free agents, unrestrained by enforceable laws, inevitably come into conflict with one another, conflict which if left to follow its natural course turns violent and lethal. Potentially, we are always in a condition of "war of all against all" in which "the life of man is solitary, poor, nasty, brutish and short." (Hobbes:1651:1962:100.) We can only escape from this anarchic condition in which we are all permanently and mortally vulnerable to one another, if we agree to surrender a portion of our natural liberty to do whatever we like to some sovereign body, who will make and enforce rules under which we must all live. Only in this way can we effectively protect ourselves from the depredations to which we would otherwise be vulnerable at the hands of our fellow human beings, exercising their own unbridled free choices in pursuit of their own desires. From this it follows that it is rational, because in our real interests, to relinquish our freedom to a government, to the extent that this is necessary to enable us to live peaceably and securely. But it is only rational to do this in so far as other people are willing to do the same. Thus, for example, we give up our freedom to get what we want through looting, rapine, pillage and murder if others will do the same.

Hobbes is rightly called "the first liberal" in that his central claim is that the existence, constitution and activities of government can only be rationally justified to the extent that they secure the conditions for the exercise of maximum individual freedom: it is a minimalist doctrine because it holds that we should have as little government as is possible, consistent with the requirements of peace. In fact Hobbes thinks that that minimum amount of government will have to be very large indeed: the state will need to be a "Leviathan". Nor will it be possible, according to Hobbes, to accommodate the cardinal liberal virtue of tolerance, especially with respect to religious and political convictions. Tolerance of diverse views in these areas, Hobbes believes, leads to that greatest of all political evils: civil war. Nevertheless, the liberal principle of equal freedoms is clearly entrenched in Hobbes's system, because the law may only prevent someone from doing as they choose if it also prevents everyone else from doing the same thing. Further, such abridgements of liberty can only be justified if it can be shown that, without them, people would be less able to do what they choose and that with them, everyone will come closer to being able to enjoy the greatest possible amount of freedom to determine how they will live.

From this follows a second political implication of liberal anthropology. This often goes under the title "the Rule of Law". By definition, all laws violate individual autonomy, since laws are are not self-imposed but imposed on us from outside.[3] If these violations are to be legitimated according to the equal freedom principle, then the laws must be made and applied impersonally and impartially: impersonally, meaning that they are indifferent to the wishes or interests of any particular person or group of persons; impartially, in that they are binding on all the members of the community where they hold sway and admit of no difference of treatment as between persons whose situations are the

3. "Autonomy" comes from the Greek "*autos*" = "self" and "*nomos*" = "law." Autonomy may therefore be thought of, paraphrasing Lincoln on democracy, as government of oneself, by oneself and for oneself.

same. This is what is commonly understood in locutions like "no-one is above the law," "the governance of laws, not the governance of men," "no discrimination on irrelevant grounds such as race, gender, class, creed etc." and "like cases to be treated alike." The realities are of course much more complicated and contentious than these slogans suggest, but most of us do not find the ideal of equality or equal rights before the law hard to comprehend and we certainly have little difficulty in identifying situations in which this principle of justice is breached.

We are now in a position to spell out somewhat more precisely the relations between liberalism and democracy. Three issues in particular need to be clarified. First, the way in which democracy and liberalism may conflict with one another; second the way in which they are generally, but by no means invariably supportive of one another as a matter of contingent fact; third, the way in which some aspects of liberalism necessarily, whether causally or as a matter of logic, entail some aspects of democracy and vice versa.

First, then, we should note that, provided the law secures individual liberty for all equally, it does not matter how the law is made or by whom. Monarchs can govern liberally as well as elected assemblies; sometimes they may do so better. It is an error, which does no service to the cause of democracy, to think that every decision democratically arrived at is necessarily a good decision, whether from a liberal point of view or any other. Nor are decisions about communal policy only good or liberal if they are democratically made. Majorities can be, and often are, illiberal and wrong; minorities may be liberal and right. Moreover democracy contains an especially dangerous threat to liberal values when it comes to the treatment of individuals and minorities. This threat has long been identified by liberal theorists such as Montesquieu, Madison, de Tocqueville and J.S. Mill as the threat of a "tyranny of the majority."

On the other hand — and this is the second isssue — as a matter of empirical fact, it does seem to be the case that societies which are governed with an element of democracy are, in fact, more protective of individual liberties than are societies where all power is in the hands of an autocrat or a minority elite. This is inspite of the tendency of bureaucracies in modern democracies (mainly as a consequence of the sheer number of people they have to deal with) to ride roughshod over the rights of individuals and groups who are weak.

That democracy tends to secure individual rights better than other forms of government might seem to be contradicted in the case of deeply divided societies like Northern Ireland, Israel, Sri Lanka, South Africa and many others where, in practice, one-person-one-vote elections would, or do, lead to the exclusion of permanent minorities from all political power. This, however, seems to be an illusion which results from neglect of the last part of the formula for democratic elections: one-person-one-vote-one-value. The problem of ensuring that permanent minorities are not permanently impotent is partly one of ensuring that there are certain things which may not be done to individuals or groups, even if the doing of them is desired by the majority. Most commonly, a constitution must protect civil rights against any government no matter how popular. The other part of the problem is one of ensuring, typically through systems of proportional representation, that the votes of some do not count less than equally, or even for nothing, relative to those of others.

Finally, we need to note where there are necessary connections between liberalism and democracy. These are of two types: those which concern the mechanics of democracy and those which concern values. Because democracy, by its nature, presupposes the tolerance of possible opposition to the government, a number of freedoms are, in practice, indispensable as instruments for making legitimate opposition possible. These include freedom of speech and the press, freedom of assembly and of political association, and the right to vote and to run for office in fair elections.

The necessity here is causal or practical: one could imagine a world in which the people exercised ultimate power over their rulers without these institutions, but in practice, in the world as it actually is, this cannot be done. The other type of necessary relation which subsists between liberalism and democracy is less obvious. It consists in the fact that democracy is the only system of government which treats all adults as being equally entitled to an equal say in determining matters of public policy.

It is a matter of the meaning of the term that democracy is a system of government in which people have equal power to determine the behaviour of their government. This means that they are equally free (or unfree) to decide what happens to them as a consequence of politics. What this equal freedom means we shall need to consider when we examine socialism, for much socialist criticism of liberals focuses on the claim that, on the liberal conception and under liberal institutions, there is no real equality or freedom.

Here, however, we need to state what in essence it is that a liberal democrat believes and what, consequently, are the ideological beliefs which, according to the TOLD thesis, have been vindicated by the collapse of Communism. The two core convictions of democratic liberalism are that: we should be should be as little subject as possible to the decisions of any government, but where we must be subject to such decisions we should all be equally able to determine what those decisions are. But what, on the liberal account, is the justification for a politics based on these convictions? The answer is somewhat surprising or, at least, different from what is often supposed. For the liberal claim that we are all equally free does not yield the conclusion that people are always, or even typically, the best judges of their own interests. Manifestly many of us, much of the time, are not. For this reason, as well no doubt as for others, it does not follow that treating people equally as free agents will necessarily lead to the greatest happiness of the greatest number, or to the triumph of wisdom and goodness, however conceived. Any libertarian would have to concede that the exercise of free choice has led, historically, to political tragedies of epic proportions. Modern liberals, with the appalling experience of the twentieth century behind them are, as we shall see in considering Pluralism, typically sceptical about the prospects for dramatically improving the human condition and hostile to any claim that progress towards utopia is even possible, let alone inevitable.

It might then be thought that the best that can be said in favour of liberal democracy is that it constitutes in practice the best damage control machinery we possess, and/or that it is the least bad of a number of political evils. But a more formidable argument for the liberal view holds that governments ought to treat all their subjects as if they were the best judges of how they should live, even though they are frequently not. This is because not to do so is to relegate them to a condition of permanent moral infantility. Thus the toughest justification for democratic liberalism rests on the claim that individuals should have the freedom to decide how they will conduct their lives, not because this will make them happy or virtuous, but because such treatment uniquely accords with their dignity as moral agents, that is, as fully-fledged persons and not as children or animals or mere things.

CHAPTER FIVE

COMMUNISM

Liberalism begins with a repudiation of absolutism as irrational, tyrannical and unjust. Socialism begins with the charge that liberalism is itself born of a form of irrationality, which breeds tyranny and injustice at least as oppressive as that which it claimed to replace. At the heart of the charge is the claim that liberals fail to understand the real importance of money in human affairs, for it is the inequitable distribution of money and other resources which, according to socialists, is the root cause of all human unfreedom. And the reason why liberals fail to notice this is that they have a vested material interest in not noticing it.

The most radical and, in that way as well as others, the most interesting version of this thesis is Marxian communism. This is also clearly the account which is most immediately relevant to the evaluation of the TOLD thesis. However, in addition to addressing the Marxian account, it is necessary to say something about non-Marxian, reformist socialism which I shall call "social-democratism." This is necessary partly because otherwise the nature and basis of Marx's radicalism cannot be properly appreciated, and partly because it is important in considering the future of ideology after Communism to take account of the possibility that what will supersede Communism, and perhaps Capitalism as well, will be some form of non-Marxian socialism. Perhaps, indeed, this has already happened.

As we have seen the metaphysics of liberalism require respect for the freedom of all people to determine how they will live and what goals they will pursue. The principal obstacles in the way of meeting this requirement which confronted the early liberals, often also called the "classical" liberals, were hereditary power and privilege rather than property. The individual's freedom to try to live what he or she considered to be a desirable kind of life was drastically curtailed or even eliminated for the overwhelming majority of people by the accident of birth. Social rank and all the benefits and/or burdens which accompanied it were held to reflect the will of God, who also desired and decreed that these ranks be transmitted from generation to generation. In theory, there could (except under highly exceptional circumstances) be no "social mobility," that is movement from between the ranks, for example between peasant or serf and noble lord or lady. In practice, also, social rank determined who did and who did not own the fundamental source of all wealth, namely land.

But it was not the unequal distribution of wealth as such, nor even the existence under feudalism[1] of severe and widespread poverty, which fuelled and focused (at least consciously) early liberal hostility to the whole system. It was rather the fact that the lives of individuals under this system were directed and controlled not by the individuals themselves but by their social superiors. Freedom was thus first and foremost a matter of curbing the power which some people could exercise over others, with special reference to the power to kill, imprison, torture and expropriate. The goal of the liberal struggle was thus equal protection for all through governance under just and rational laws, rather than at the arbitrary discretion of often unjust men and women: equality of opportunity and access to the good things of life, including, not only private property but also education and the more desirable occupations, was a secondary matter, which,

1. I use "feudalism" in a very wide sense to refer to societies where the primary economic activity is agriculture; where peasants and serfs work the land for its hereditary owners; where political power is well-nigh absolute and resides exclusively in the hands of the land-owning class; and where radical inegalitarianism is legitimated by eschatological religion, adherence to which is compulsory. Feudalism in this broad sense includes not only the arrangements of mediaeval society but also those of the period of absolute monarchies in Europe. This is consonant with what Marx himself understood by feudalism.

when it was considered at all, was seen (and still is) as a necessary corollary of individual liberty.

The feudal system was, no doubt, more burdensome the further down the social scale one found oneself, but the educated and prosperous bourgeoisie were quite as vulnerable to drastic penalties for incurring aristocratic displeasure as were the peasantry. On the other hand, the bourgeoisie had a powerful interest in preserving inequalities of income and wealth. Notoriously, it was the bourgeoisie who made the great liberal revolutions in England (1688), in America (1776) and in France (1789)[2].

In reality, the degree of wretchedness which feudalism caused to those who lived under it varied considerably, depending on how benign or cruel was the behaviour of individual members of the classes more privileged and powerful than your own. It should also be noted that the feudal system was neither as rigid nor as tyrannical as it appeared to its liberal critics. Common law rights, owing much to Roman justice, were often effective in securing fundamental liberties for even the base-born. Official religion, although a major partner in feudal tyranny, did offer everyone some further protections as illustrated, for example, by the institution of giving "sanctuary." There was, moreover, something of a system of checks and balances consequent upon the separated powers of Church, Aristocracy and sovereign monarch. In practice, too, avenues for upward mobility were provided for the intellectually gifted by the Church, and for those with the appropriate prowess, through military service, domestic and foreign, mercenary or conscript.

---

2. On my understanding, the French Revolution was not only, and perhaps not primarily a liberal revolution. The calls for equality and, still more, for fraternity were in principle radically socialist. But the liberal component, which consisted in getting rid of the arbitrary power of the monarchy, the aristocracy and the Church in the name of "Liberty" was not less prominent, and, arguably, it was only this liberal component which the Revolution was successful in securing. Equality and fraternity as ideals, were realised neither during nor after the Revolution, which most obviously constituted a triumph for the bourgeois class over the aristocracy. This, again, coincides with how Marx saw the Revolution.

Nevertheless, the achievement of liberal political theory and practice in much of Europe and in North America between, say, 1688 and 1870, was the establishment of constitutional governments which were committed to protecting equal liberty before the law. This liberty, however, was "negative" liberty in the sense which Isaiah Berlin has made famous: it prescribed what people, and especially rulers, could not do to anyone by way of preventing them from living and acting as they chose. But it did not ensure that everyone was free, in the substantial sense of actually being able to live the kind of life that they either in fact wanted to live, or would have wanted to live, if they had been fully rational.

By the beginning of the nineteenth century, however, under what was, in many ways, the devastating human and social impact of industrialisation, it was already clear that negative liberty alone was insufficient to generate justice, general prosperity or universal happiness, despite what some liberal apologists of capitalism were wont to claim, then as now. That liberalism offers only formal, or theoretical, or legal freedom rather than "real," "true" and "actual" freedom is the essential charge levelled against it by all socialists, whether Marxian or non-Marxian. For what was glaringly apparent about those societies which made the transition from absolute to constitutionally limited government, from feudalism to liberal capitalism, from monarchy and oligarchy to a degree of democracy, was their utter failure to relieve the miserable conditions in which the vast majority of their citizens were compelled to live.

As the ideological dominion of liberalism grew in power and scope, so did the extensiveness and intensity of poverty. No-one has documented more meticulously and more heart-rendingly than Marx himself the suffering inflicted on the vast majority of people by the operations of what he called "Capitalism," whose ruling ideology he identified as liberalism and whose system of government was so-called "representative democracy".

The paradigm case of this suffering, decisive against any claim that Victorian capitalism might be compatible with either freedom or justice, Marx took to be the extreme child abuse inherent in a system which encouraged child labour. In *Capital* for example, Marx offers us this glimpse of the workings of the lace trade: "Children of nine or ten are dragged from their squalid beds at two, three, four o'clock in the morning and compelled to work for a bare subsistence until ten, eleven or twelve at night, their limbs dwindling, their faces whitening, and their humanity sinking utterly into a stone-like torpor, quite horrible to contemplate." (Marx:1867:1938:227-8.)

But child labour was only the supreme evil in which the whole horrible system culminated. For the inexorable logic of capitalist economics condemns "the vast majority of people" — men, women and children — to a slavery quite as wretched and morally outrageous as that practised in the American cotton fields. This happens because the essence of capitalism is that it is a system which allows, and indeed encourages individuals to accumulate as much private property as possible. This liberal, apparently innocuous and certainly not obviously iniquitous approach to private property in fact produces slavery for the masses, because it allows a minority of people to own between them all the means of producing wealth in society, notably raw materials and industrial plant. Because this (bourgeois) minority own all the capital, they control everyone else's ability to survive. Owning no capital themselves, the (proletarian) masses can only live at all by selling their labour to the capitalists for whatever the capitalists are willing to pay. In practice, this is always the barest minimum necessary to enable the worker to go on working in such a way as to maximise the capitalist owner's profits. When the worker's wages are no longer justifiable from the point of view of the capitalist's economic interests as calculated in terms of the ratio of costs to benefits, the wages are lowered or the worker dismissed.

At this point it might be objected by a champion of liberalism that the misery, degradation and exploitation of working-class life under early industrialisation was eliminated in capitalist societies on the basis of arguments which, far from conflicting with liberal principles, in fact relied on them. Thus, the kind of institutionalised child abuse which Marx and others identified is incompatible with liberal political principles because, on the one hand, children have not reached the age of reason when they are able and entitled to enter freely into contracts. On the other, it is the parents who, in compelling their children to go out to work, are violating the children's rights as autonomous persons. If the parents themselves are forced to do this because of their own poverty, then the state may, on liberal grounds, intervene to prevent that poverty from resulting in a violation of the freedom of children. The government, therefore, may and must use its coercive power to prevent parents from sending their children out to work and employers from conniving in this form of slavery. If this means that the state must also provide the funds out of taxation for ensuring that children and their families do not starve as a result, so be it.

Moreover, whether the principles involved were, strictly speaking, liberal or not, the lot of the working-class generally could be, and some would argue was, sufficiently improved by reform within the system. The revolutionary methods which Marx thought indispensable for the creation of a truly good and just society, or the communist ideal of overthrowing the entire capitalist system by abolishing private property, were both therefore unnecessary. The kind of fundamental reforms from within, which both liberals and non-Marxist socialists worked for and continue to work for, in reaction against the iniquities and sufferings that Marx and others so vigorously identified, have most notably included: better pay and working conditions, including leisure and pension rights and protection from unemployment; equality of opportunity through the outlawing of dis criminatory practices and the extension of access to education to everyone, regardless of whether they or their families can afford it; the provision, from taxation, to the poor, of basic welfare, notably shelter, medical services and a minimum disposable income, or its equivalent, in vouchers for food, clothing etc; and the political empowering of the working class through the Trade Union movement, the extension of the franchise and the formation of labour-supporting political parties which could successfully compete in democratic elections.

All this, so it might be argued, has been accomplished, by and large in Western democracies which have eschewed experiments with communism. And people's perceptions of whether this claim is true or not is, perhaps, the single most decisive factor in determining what they think of the TOLD thesis; that is, whether or not they think that the collapse of Communism betokens or confirms the triumph of liberal democracy, as the West (when it is being coherent) understands both democracy and liberalism. The persistence of poverty in the ex-Communist world is also now dissipating initial enthusiasm for Capitalism and constitutes there a grave and continuing threat to the protection and promotion of liberal and democratic institutions.

In this kind of argument, the distinction between liberals and reformist or welfare socialists risks becoming blurred to a quibble. For if the state is obliged to compel some people to pay taxes in order to secure the material conditions for other people to enjoy freedom, then the pure liberal claim that the state may only intervene to prevent one citizen from infringing on the liberty of another becomes unsustainable, or at least in need of drastic reinterpretation. Roughly, the classical liberal insists on a minimum of constraints by government, or anyone else, on what individuals may do. Welfare socialists stress that the range of choices which are in fact open to people must be extended, through education and an adequate availability of money and leisure. It is, however, unclear that being unfree to pursue a career of one's choice because one is legally discriminated against, differs in kind from being unfree to do the same thing because one's parents can't or won't pay for the necessary studies.

In both cases it seems clear that the state should intervene, and it doesn't seem to make any difference whether this is seen as a matter of preventing unfair exclusion or of securing everybody's chance of inclusion. This is no doubt why, irritatingly, the word "liberal" in American has come to mean roughly what "socialist" means in Europe. It is also why, historically, people have wanted to classify nineteenth century liberals such as T.H.Green as "new liberals", because they argued that a pure doctrine of non-interventionism could not meet the moral requirements of a society where unearned poverty was widespread.

However, for present purposes, at least, it is more helpful to ignore any putative distinction between "old" and "new" liberals in the British context, as well as that between American and English terminology. Thus, as I shall use the terms, the essential differences between classical liberalism, social-democratism and

Marxian communism are given in their conceptions of the relations between individual liberty and equality.

The liberal, as we have seen, holds that social arrangements are just to the extent that they maximise equal liberty for all individuals, and that injustice is to be equated with violations of individual liberty. The social-democrat, however, claims that a fully free, (liberal) market system produces endemic poverty amongst the weakest members of society who are, through no fault of their own, unable to compete for the money necessary to live a decent human life. The existence of this poverty means one or more of three things. Either liberal freedoms are, in reality although not in theory, denied to some people in all societies and to the majority of people in most societies; or these merely legal freedoms — from naked coercion and official discrimination — are worthless to the poor; or political liberty, as conceived by liberals is, at most, only one among a number of competing values, including equality and a minimum level of prosperity, which must be, as far as possible, harmonised within a just society. And of these values individual liberty is not always the most important.

The Marxian communist view differs as radically from social-democratism as it does from liberalism. For this view which was first articulated, not by Marx but by Rousseau, holds that inequality in society is the fundamental cause of real unfreedom for all. Here freedom is understood, not merely as being unable to live as one might wish, because one lacks the material means to do so, but in terms of the blinding, crippling and paralysing of the human spirit, which makes it impossible for people even to aspire to, let alone achieve, the living of a truly fulfilling and fulfilled human life. For Rousseau and Marx, the institution of private property inexorably leads to inequality and is the source of all social misery. It produces radical intellectual deception and self-deception, and issues in moral corruption in every sphere of human interaction, private as well as public.

This is because inequality makes people dependent on one another and so breeds cowardice and cruelty, meanness and greed, vanity and hypocrisy, servility and arrogance. Private property and its unequal distribution also lead to the enslavement of rich and poor alike, because the (idle and incompetent) rich lack self-sufficiency and are wholly dependent on the services of the poor who hate them and would kill them if they could. Meanwhile, the poor must (abjectly) serve the rich if they are to survive. Both are enslaved, at a yet deeper level, by their addiction to the material unnecessities which money can buy: the love of luxury for Rousseau, the "fetishism of commodities" for Marx.

Crucial to Marx's argument is that what workers receive as wages is far less than the value of the work they perform, as measured by the difference between the price which owners eventually receive for the goods produced and the totality of the costs to them of completing the production process — purchase of raw materials, overheads, transportation, the wages themselves etc.. This makes capitalism not only a system of concealed slavery, because the workers cannot really choose whether to work or not on the terms laid down by the capitalists, but also exploitative, because the workers are robbed of the fruits of their labours.

However, the heart and genius of Marx's assault on capitalism consists, not in his analysis of either the inequities of distribution which capitalism entrenches, or the material wretchedness which it fosters among the propertyless. It consists rather in his insight into what capitalism does to the humanity of human beings and to the relations between them and the world they inhabit. The central concept here is "alienation."[3]

Under capitalism, according to Marx, human beings become alienated from their work, from one another, from themselves and from the natural order. Work is not an expression and extension of creative human personality: it is mechanical, impersonal,

3. There is a fair measure of antipathy to this term amongst both Marxist and non-Marxist scholars. The Right tend to sneer at it in the same way as they sneer at a term like "Existential angst": it seems pretentious, vague, implausible and murky. The Left dislike the thought that an idea which seems so soft-boiled should have featured centrally in the work of one to be admired as much for his social scientific hard-headedness as for his revolutionary toughness and roughness. It seems to me indisputable, however, that what Marx meant by "alienation" is both clear and central to his communism.

dehumanising and hateful drudgery. The workers do not see other workers as congenial collaborators but as dangerous competitors for their jobs; and in the capitalist bourgeois they see, not a fellow human being, but only a literally inhuman tyrant. Moreover, workers come to see themselves as mere machines, like those with which they work, not as persons but as things. They are alienated in consequence from their biological nature — family life is "ripped asunder" in industrial society — and from the world of nature which becomes merely the repository of raw materials to be exploited.

Nor, and this is a crucial point, is it only the workers who are afflicted by alienation under capitalism. The members of the bourgeois class are also estranged from fulfilling work; they are also enemies and competitors to one another and are compelled to live in a condition of fear and hostility towards the vast, impersonal, proletarian masses. They, too, are dehumanised and denatured, in that (for Marx) supremely contemptible institution, the bourgeois family, which transforms women and children into mere instruments of production and labour.

It is important to emphasise that Marx does not blame the capitalist bourgeoisie for being as they are. Blame would be inappropriate, since we are dealing here, not with the vicious choices of individual exploiters, but with the working out of a historical drama, driven by economic forces over which individuals have no control. Moreover, the individual actors in this drama know not what they do: they are blinded by ideology, which causes them sincerely to believe that there is a universal morality which requires them to behave in a manner which, in fact, only serves the interests of the ruling class. This comes about because what we believe with respect to morality and religion, as well as the legal and political arrangements which we acknowledge to be just, emerges in response to the material circumstances of the society in which we live.

At its most fundamental, human life is concerned with working in order to secure the means to survive. As human evolution and technological progress advance, so the division of labour develops and the institution of private property becomes established: a few own, the many are more or less explicitly owned; most work, the minority are worked for. This produces socio-economic classes, ranged always into two broad and necessarily antagonistic categories: the exploiters and exploited, the dominant and the dominated, the haves and the have-nots. Everything depends on who, in any particular society, owns the means of production — land in pre-industrial societies, factories and raw materials in industrial Europe. For owners of the means of production, that is of the basic necessities for generating any wealth at all, are able, by threatening to withhold what is required for mere survival, to appropriate, in the form of huge profits, the surplus value of other people's work. It is in order to secure the hegemony of the property-owning classes that all the trappings of tyranny are introduced into society: repressive laws brutally enforced, extensive indoctrination and propaganda, and the merciless suppression of anyone who seeks to tell the truth about the system and to set the broad masses of the people free.

The fact that tyranny emerges, not out of individual wickedness, but from the historical unfolding of impersonal economic forces, means that it can only be overthrown by the forcible seizing of power by the oppressed majority. It cannot be accomplished by appealing to the moral conscience of the oppressors and exhorting them to reform. There must be a revolution in which they are dispossessed and for the first time ever the masses, rather than a minority, take ownership and control of the means of production; and it is the task and destiny of the Communist Party to accomplish this revolution. After the revolution this party — which Lenin called the "vanguard of the revolution", and Marx saw as the vehicle through which "the dictatorship of the proletariat" would be exercised — must govern so as to ensure that a transition is made to a society which has no classes, because no-one has the kind of private property rights which enable them to exploit and enslave others. Once this classless society has been achieved, there will be no further need for a state, since the only function of states is to regulate class conflict in the interests of the dominant class. No classes means no class conflict and no need for a state armed with coercive powers to contain and control class conflict. Consequently the state will "wither away."

The drama of human history would be a tragedy in the classical manner were it not for the fact that Marx anticipates this wholly happy ending. He bases his optimism on his conviction that the conflict between bourgeoisie and proletariat, when it is concluded, will not, like all previous class conflicts, issue in a new antagonism between a dominating and dominated class. What we are witnessing now, and indeed participating in, is the class war to end all class wars. In this way Marx's theory is itself an "end-of-History" and an "end-of-ideology" thesis. It is, therefore, ironic that we should be now considering whether the collapse of a political system, purportedly based on Marx's teachings, is most accurately to be interpreted as betokening the decisive ideological triumph of the very democratic, liberal capitalism which Marx thought he had shown to be doomed — exposed as an iniquitous and tyrannical sham, considerably more brutalising and cruel than the feudalism which it had replaced!

The obvious move for a loyal Marxist to make at this point is to deny that Soviet Communism had anything to do with Marxian communism, except as a grisly travesty. On this view, the Russian revolution was hijacked, possibly by Lenin, certainly by Stalin, who, far from continuing the commitment to create a truly communist society, merely replaced the old Czarist oligarchy with a new, privileged and tyrannical elite of *apparatchiks*. And something similar must go for the other revolutions and regimes which have been instigated in the name of Communism, notably in China but also throughout much of the Third world including Cuba and, briefly but appallingly, Kampuchea. This kind of apologetics is of the same type that world religions are compelled to engage when the blood has dried after a particularly gruesome episode of religiously instituted evil. The Inquisition is the classic example.

However, a communist who takes this kind of line in the face of what has happened in countries which have called themselves "Communist," confronts a major difficulty. For if the argument is that, as with Christianity, the only thing wrong with communism is that it has never been tried, then the question arises of whether the doctrine ever could be put into practice.

Here Marxian communists are not in the same position as early Christians who were simply wrong in predicting the imminence of the Second Coming. The Christians can coherently claim that

God's will is, in large measure, inscrutable, partly at least because otherwise freedom of choice for human beings would be impossible. Consequently, "No man knoweth the hour" when the Kingdom of Heaven will arrive and History come to an end. Moreover, and more decisively, Christianity makes the advent of utopia conditional to a large degree on people's moral choices and on the effectiveness of a missionary church in transforming the way people live and think. The end of Christian History, therefore, depends on human choices. But with Marxism, the argument cannot be that communism would work if only it were espoused and implemented by people of wisdom and good will. For under Capitalism, according to Marx, it is impossible for the overwhelming majority of people to develop good will and wisdom: their economic circumstances render them cruel, greedy, selfish and, above all, blind about where their true interests lie and how these can best be secured. Utopia is thus dependent on capitalism's collapsing in the radical and comprehensive manner which Marx predicted. Furthermore, for Marx, the post-revolutionary phase must be a dictatorship exercised by an enlightened elite in the interests of the people, rather than by the people as a whole acting directly or through elected representatives. Following Hegel, Marx thought political developments were not a matter of how individuals and groups exercised their free will and, as such, in principle, unpredictable: it was a matter of the unfolding of historical necessities. But if this is so, then it becomes a very serious objection to Marxism that things have not in fact unfolded as Marx predicted they would.

Thus, in capitalist countries, revolutions have not occurred as the proletarian poor grew poorer, more numerous, more embittered and better equipped, as a consequence of education, to prosecute a successful revolution. The development of the capitalist system has not led to its "collapsing under the weight of its own internal contradictions" as both the motivation and the ability to revolt of the most numerous class have progressively increased in response to the demands of capitalism itself. Instead, the workers of the world have, on the whole, opted to seek to reform the system from within representative democracies, and to ameliorate their material circumstances though powerful Trades Unions and the establishment of generous welfare states. Thus far, at least, and despite the fact that areas of material wretchedness persist in capitalist societies, working-class movements have been very effective, certainly more so than Marx would have thought possible. For better or worse, the proletariat of the industrial West has not said: "Give me liberty or give me death." It has said: "We'll take the money".

A consequence of this, however, is that the claim that Marxism has been falsified, because what it predicted has not happened, will not provide the straightforward vindication of capitalism that some capitalists have wanted to extract from it. Thus, it is common for critics of Marxism to say that the theory of communism was falsified by events, because capitalism did not collapse as Marx foretold, but instead continues to flourish and, indeed, has recently demonstrated beyond all doubt its superiority over Communism as a means of securing liberty and generating prosperity. But this is both too simple and too smug. For what has, at least arguably, happened is that Capitalism in the sense in which Marx understood the term, has indeed collapsed, but what it has been replaced by is a form of non-Marxist, non-revolutionary, "mixed economy," welfare-state socialism, for which the least misleading and inconvenient label is "social-democratism." We must now therefore consider, in general, the nature of this ideology and, in particular whether it can be adequately disentangled from both democratic liberalism and Marxism in order to stake a convincing claim to the allegiance of the post-Communist world.

CHAPTER SIX

SOCIAL-DEMOCRATISM

The economies of modern industrial societies are not driven or dominated by the owners of private capital. Economic power is overwhelmingly in the hands of managers in both the public and private sectors. The legal owners of capital are ironically for the most part workers who hold insurance policies, contribute to pension funds and, where industries are subsidised or owned by the state, pay taxes. The number of people who live on the income from inherited wealth is very small, as is the number of individual entrepreneurs who become wealthy by starting their own companies. Those who are really rich in modern societies are those who typically work for companies listed on the stock exchanges and receive very large remuneration packages. Nor are the horrors of poverty which Marx documented still a feature of modern industrial society. There are other horrors certainly, but these are more likely to spring, not from conditions of employment, but from unemployment and unemployability.

Some people who think of themselves as classical liberals and call themselves "libertarians" deplore this collapse of capitalism and its replacement with a high degree of state regulation of the economy. Most socialists of all descriptions remain profoundly dissatisfied by the inequalities which persist under what they would still describe as capitalism, although they would now identify as the source of economic tyranny and injustice, not private ownership of the means of production, but the power of the giant multi-national corporation.

The point remains that the societies of the West do not operate according to the principles of liberal capitalism as Marx described them, any more than the Soviet Union operated according to what he understood to be the principles of genuine socialism, let alone communism.

Are we to conclude from this that the TOLD-thesis should be amended, so as to propose that what we are witnessing with the collapse of Communism is the culmination of a process which has been going on in the United States since the New Deal, and in Europe since 1945, and which should be accounted the triumph, not of liberal, but of social(ist) democracy?

The answer to this question depends on whether this ideology is intrinsically coherent and credible and so able to furnish the basis for enduring political institutions and practice.

The principal reason for thinking that social-democratism, rather than democratic liberalism, is the ideology which has finally triumphed with the collapse of Communism and the end of the Cold War, is that in the so-called "Capitalist" countries of the West, social-democratism is in fact the currently dominant ideology, and this notwithstanding the apparently successful inroads made into it by the "neo-conservatism" of, most notably, the Reagan and Thatcher regimes. Thus, no-one seeking elective office can afford to doubt that it is the business of the state to raise taxes in order to fund welfare services. The principle that those who can afford to help the poor and the weak should be compelled to do so by the state, is no longer seriously disputed in the practical politics of the industrialised West. What is hotly disputed, within and between different Western countries, is the empirical question of how most effectively to improve the circumstances of the poor and weak.

In particular the question is vigorously disputed whether this is best done through the assumption of responsibility by central and local governments for providing such services as schooling, health-care, "social work," housing, unemployment insurance, and pensions; or whether government would do better simply to see to it that people can afford such of these services as are deemed necessary and which otherwise they could not afford. The principle that people should not have to forego medical care, education, shelter etc. because of poverty is not in dispute. Even the most free of free market economists like Hayek and Milton Friedman agree that it is a legitimate function of the state[1] to provide a "safety net" for those who would otherwise and undeservedly crash, perhaps literally to their deaths, in modern capitalist societies. There is also, of course, considerable disagreement about how high or low this safety net should be placed, as well as about how tight the mesh needs to be in order to ensure that nobody (who shouldn't) falls through it. These are disputes about what constitutes the basic necessities of life and how best to secure them for everyone: they are not disputes about ultimate political norms or values.

This point, about disputes about facts versus disputes about values, needs to be generalised. For the reality is that the overwhelming majority of political disagreements are not, despite the rhetoric in which they are couched, about issues of moral principle: they are about matters of empirical fact. In particular, they are about the likely consequences of doing this rather than that, and about the best means of achieving commonly agreed ends.

Thus the elimination of poverty, justice for all, individual liberty (in some sense at least), the eradication of violent crime, domestic and international peace, the maximisation of happiness (again in some sense), are all very widely and quite deeply shared values in the modern Western world, even if there are important variations in the way they are interpreted; and the real differences between competing democratic parties concerns what policies will best protect and promote these values, with,

---

1. In the intriguing case of Japan, welfare "from cradle to grave" is principally provided by companies rather than by the state. This might seem to compel qualification, at least, of the claim that Japan is ideologically similar to the more geographically identified countries of the West. However the important point is that in Japan, as elsewhere, it is taken as axiomatic that the rich and strong must look after the weak and poor with respect to basic needs. The fact that in Japan the relevant welfare services are paid for by business directly rather than by government using taxes raised from the beneficiaries of profitable business is, from an ideological point of view, a detail. More needs to be said about Japan in connection with nationalism.

possibly, some difference of emphasis about their relative importance when they conflict.[2]

The reason why this very large measure of agreement about political values is obscured and, instead, essentially pragmatic political disputes are represented as conflicts about issues of fundamental moral principle, is a matter for the psychology of political competition. In order for politicians to win popular support, they need both to dramatise and to moralise the differences between themselves and their opponents. In particular they need to portray their opponents as not simply mistaken but as evil or at least mad. Otherwise domestic populaces or, in the case of international relations, potential members of the nation's defence forces, will see that the real differences between the competing politicians are marginal, difficult to judge and morally finely balanced. Consequently circumstances do not in fact offer them a clear-cut choice, which they have a duty to make one way rather than another, because it is a choice between wise and holy virtue and insane, diabolical vice.

However, the fact that there is consensus about values, not only amongst those who won the war against Communism, but also — to a large extent — amongst their former foes, is not enough to vindicate the view that social-democratism has now decisively triumphed and is destined increasingly to be acknowledged as the common ideology of the whole world, developed and developing. And indeed there are at least two decisive reasons for thinking that social-democratism, as an ideology, is neither credible nor coherent.

The first is empirical and relates to bureaucratisation.

One of the most obvious and perhaps the most fundamental of the failures of Communism in Russia was that, far from initiating a withering away of the state, it ushered in a Leviathan-like bureaucratic tyranny. Literally everything came to be controlled

2. It is this, rather than any false thesis about human behaviour being determined in the same way as that of material objects, which makes possible the activity of social science.

by civil servants who owed their appointment and advancement primarily to political acceptability rather than ability to perform a job with demonstrable skill. The same phenomenon contributed substantially to the defeat of Nazi Germany and has been responsible for the failures of many newly independent "developing" countries in fact to develop as they could and should have. Quite apart from the appalling cruelty which it breeds, any system which ties power and prosperity to the political skills which make for success in party politics, is inherently so inefficient economically that, typically, it can survive only by instituting slave labour.[3]

Social-democratism, as it has operated in the West since the Second World War, has been nowhere near as barbarous as this, despite the rhetoric of the radically disaffected. Nevertheless, the inefficiency and inhumanity of bureaucratic tyranny have been sufficiently in evidence under social-democratism as to have seriously discredited this ideology in the West. Hence the "neo-conservative" successes of the eighties, which were really unsuccessful attempts to revive liberal minimalism by "getting government off the back of the people."

The existence of multi-party democracy and a strong private sector in Western countries have done much to curb the power of permanent government officials to plunder and tyrannise those they govern. These institutions have the great merit of allowing alternative ways of doing things to be tested against experience.

For example, the fallacy that if industries are nationalised, and run by civil servants answerable to democratically elected politicians, then these industries will be run in the public interest, rather than for the benefit of a handful of selfish individuals, has been thoroughly exposed. Civil servants answerable to political masters are not personally less selfish or self-interested than managers answerable to share-holders. Why should they be? The difference is that where managers must make profits, political appointees must garner votes; and it is a brutal fact that what is profitable is often not generally popular. Hence, nationalised

3. Genocide is another extreme solution to the problem of too many mouths to feed.

industries are well-nigh doomed to be run unprofitably, from the point of view of promoting the interests of society as a whole. It is, unfortunately not yet clear that de-nationalised or privatised industry can be run profitably in this sense either, although there must be a *prima facie* case for thinking that society as a whole is more likely to benefit if those responsible for supplying goods and services get rewarded for pleasing their customers rather than for pleasing political masters.

However the real and unsolved problem of bureaucracy under social-democratism concerns this ideology's central institution, the welfare state. The theory of the welfare state is that it will do more effectively, thoroughly and humanely what had previously been left to private charity. This means that the provision of charity must be both professionalised and bureaucratised. Government appoints experts to ensure that people get the the things they are entitled to as a matter of fundamental human rights. This fine intention paves the road to Hell in two ways.

First, it inexorably leads to a situation where the expectations of electorates with respect to "free" welfare services outstrip what can be afforded by governments, whose incomes are (or ought to be) limited to what their electorates will put up with in terms of taxes. Hence, amongst other things, the intractability of American debt problems. Secondly and simultaneously, it leads to a proliferation of people whose careers depend precisely on the problems of the poor and weak *not* being solved. On the contrary, these problems must be (unintentionally) entrenched and the definitions of "deprivation," "disadvantage," "entitle-ment" and "rights" must be extended, which then creates work for a further large body of well-paid para-bureaucrats in the form of lawyers and professional lobbyists.

What needs to be noted here is that the apparent insolubility of welfare problems, ranging from public schooling and homeless-ness to drug-abuse and crime, may not be a function of the diffi-culty of finding ways of dealing with the problems themselves. They may, instead, be a function of the fact that they cannot be solved without imperilling the vital interests of a very large and powerful class of employees who, in many cases, are not alterna-tively employable. Add to this the enormous powers, especially of procrastination, which permanent bureaucracies must wield in competitive democracies, and the problem of getting bureaucracies to practise drastic amputative surgery on themselves turns out to be simply a modern version of the ancient problem of getting people with power to relinquish it for the public good.

It is unclear how, if at all, the multitudinous and complex problems of welfare states can be resolved, but it is worth noting that part of the problem is that much of what Marx had to say about the property-owning bourgeoisie is true in modern societies of the bureaucratic classes. They are engaged in essentially unproductive activity for which they receive excessive rewards; and they rationalise the rightness of this state of affairs to themselves with a "morality" which in fact only serves spuriously to legitimate their own power, so that they can claim to be serving the interests of those whom they are in fact tyrannising and exploiting. They do these things, not out of wickedness — their personal sincerity need not be questioned — but out of ideological blindness, induced by their membership of the dominant class in modern industrialised economies.

The problem of bureaucratisation for social-democrats is an empirical one and as such may be soluble. But social-democratism faces a conceptual or philosophical problem which seems to render the whole ideology incoherent and to force it, either to retreat into classical liberalism, or to go the whole way with Marxist communism.

At the heart of social-democratism is a concern, shared in theory by traditional liberals, with distributive justice or "fair shares." The central ideal here is equality of opportunity. This apparently unexceptionable principle asserts that in a just society no-one will be prevented from enjoying the good things of life, however identified, merely through the accident of their family circumstances, i.e. their birth and upbringing, which are factors over which they have no control and which, whether good or bad, they did nothing to deserve. It is clear, however, that these accidents are not just a matter, as in feudalism, of being born in a society where power, privilege and position are legally barred to the children of some families and reserved for those of others. Nor is it just a matter of being born poor and thereby effectively blocked, because one's parents cannot afford the requisite elite education, from gaining lucrative, high-status employment. Nor yet is the accident of birth only a matter of what has been, in the twentieth century, the most conspicuous form of discrimination, namely that based on race or gender.

If there is to be genuine equality of opportunity, then no child must be at a disadvantage for any reason of nature or nurture, when it comes to competing with others for those objects of desire of which not everyone can have as much as they would like. In practice, however, under any currently conceivable political arrangement, some children will be born and/or will grow up at a very substantial advantage relative to others in the competition for life's most popular prizes. Some parents will be more nurturing than others; some will make sacrifices for their children while others will be neglectful or exploitative; some, because of their own endowments, will be able to contribute more effectively to their children's education than others; some homes will be happier and more stable than others.

These advantages, which accrue from accidents of birth, would persist and make decisive differences even if all children underwent the same "comprehensive" schooling for the same amount of time, and extra time and money were spent on trying to remedy or compensate for the disadvantages of the unluckily born. This is because we know how much success in education is dependent on the endowments both of nature and nurture which children acquire from their parents. Moreover, at least some relative disadvantages, not all of which can be eliminated or compensated for, are a matter of being unlucky in the great genetic lottery.

The logic of social-democratic egalitarianism legitimates the use of state force to ensure that no-one is at a disadvantage as a result of pure bad luck when it comes to competing for scarce goods . If life is conceived as a race, then the social-democrat's object is to devise a system of headstarts and handicaps which will ensure that all competitors, whatever their backgrounds and whatever their physical and psychological endowments, start with the same chance of winning and being rewarded with the most coveted prizes. This is an ideal which cannot in practice be fully realised, but that is not a reason for repudiating it. For it is an ideal which can certainly be more or less closely approximated to, and the fact that something cannot be done perfectly is no reason for not trying to do it as well as possible.

However, the credibility of the social-democratic programme of promoting equality of opportunity becomes philosophically and morally suspect when we come to define what counts as luck, whether bad or good. The heart of the social-democrat's case is that the distribution of benefits and burdens in society should in no way be affected by luck. The luck in question, however, is not that which freemarket economic systems reward when, for example, people discover precious minerals on their land, or win large sums of money by gambling. Inequalities of wealth caused by luck of this sort can be fairly easily minimised, though not, perhaps, without higher costs than is generally recognised in terms of goods which are in fact humanly and socially desired and desirable: the pleasures of variety, extravagance and fantasy are examples. It is also only fairly unproblematic to agree that children with disabilities should, where possible, have access to appropriate remedial education which will enable them to catch or to keep up with their fellows. Where this is not possible, it is still unproblematic to argue that the state should use taxation to ensure that disabled people are provided with the creature comforts, as well as the basic necessities of life, which they are unable to earn for themselves.

But what about people whose bad luck consists in being congenitally idle or naturally untalented or compulsive hedonists? What about the claims of the *un*deserving poor, so brilliantly identified by Shaw's Dolittle? Are these to have the same share of the good things of life as those who are born, say, with exceptional talents for doing science or playing music, talents which have been assiduously fostered by wise and loving parents? Are such children to be allowed to benefit from their "natural" good fortune educationally and materially, or should they be deliberately handicapped? And what of those whose luck consists in being born with "good character?" Must the state treat industriousness, prudence, reliability, thrift and thoroughness, which are clearly related to the creation of wealth, as affording no claims based on desert when it comes to how that wealth is distributed?

Nor need the virtues which might be thought to deserve rewarding on the grounds of the contribution made to society, or simply on moral grounds, be "capitalist" virtues. Suppose it were agreed that unselfishness is the principal virtue which society should reward. Surely unselfishness is just as much a matter of luck as any other human quality which is a product of someone's innate disposition interacting with the environment in which they have found themselves? As such, it is no more deserving of praise and reward than other character traits. Nor should selfishness or any other vice be condemned and punished.

At this point the profoundly deterministic underskirting of social-democratic egalitarianism begins to show through. For it becomes readily apparent that there is nothing at all, whether reward or punishment, which we deserve, given that all our qualities — moral and psychological as well as physical — are products of causes or forces outside ourselves, for which we are not responsible. But this makes nonsense of the notion of fair competition, for in competitions winners are supposed to be those who demonstrate some superiority over losers on the basis of which they are deemed to deserve the prize. However, if all elements of mere luck are to be eliminated from the competition and any form of superiority is itself the product of luck, then the only fair competition can be one in which all competitors reach the winning post at the identical moment.

Marxian communists are commendably clear-sighted and consistent on this point. Marx is indeed a determinist who thinks that the activity of distributing moral praise and blame is inappropriate. His solution to the problem of equality of opportunity is to abolish the competition for scarce goods altogether, so that there are no winners or losers. Instead, competitors devote their energies and talents to melting down the prizes and distributing the common property so produced according to different people's needs, rather than their deserts, however conceived.

And indeed, logically, the only solutions to the problem for equality which results from the fact that some people, through the luck of their family circumstances, are better equipped to compete for scarce goods than others, are those proposed by communists, and notably by Plato and Marx. These are: the abolition of the family; the abolition of competition by decreeing that all scarce goods shall be communally, not privately, owned; and the transformation of people's desires through intensive compulsory education. If people can be made to want only what they can have, then the tough political problem of deciding who ought and ought not, thanks to government action or inaction, to get what they want, disappears. Equality of opportunity to become unequal in material terms immediately becomes replaced by equality of well-being for everyone.

In fact, Marx thought that, on the one hand, the communist inheritors of capitalism would be in possession of accumulated wealth and productive techniques which would render obsolete the problem of scarce material resources. On the other hand, he thought that people could be brought to reject the identification of the good things in life with the accumulation of commodities — and especially not the accumulation of more commodities than their neighbours — which is how happiness is conceived in modern consumer societies. Instead, people would work for the intrinsic satisfactions of being creative, and their relations with one another would be characterised by co-operativeness, comradeship and mutual responsibility.

Crucially absent from human motivation in Marx's communist utopia is any form of competitiveness. This commonly raises the question of whether the pursuit of communist equality is compatible with the generation of prosperity and the reduction of poverty, the argument being that competition for material advantage is a necessary ingredient in motivating people to maximum productivity. But this is an empirical claim for which, in fact, there is no empirical support, any more than there is for the claim that in an uncompetitive society people would work just as energetically as they do under competitive capitalism.

The fact is that the economic prosperity of a society does indeed depend on the totality of productive work engaged in by its work-force. But there are many ways of eliciting high productivity and offering material rewards is only one of them: others include slavery and brain-washing. Even in "capitalism" it seems that the desire for power, status and glory are often much more powerful motivators than mere greed, while envy may actually be destructive of productive work.

But the real objection to the communist pursuit of equality has to do with the drastic incursions it necessarily makes into anything ordinarily recognisable as human freedom. Hence the reluctance of social-democrats to carry their egalitarianism to its logical (communist) conclusion, which involves preventing people from doing what in fact they want to do — for example raise families and make enough money so that they can buy lots of goods and services. Moreover, laws to prevent people from doing these things, as Marx fully realised, will almost certainly be rejected if exposed to any authentically democratic decision-making procedure.

This raises what is perhaps the most fundamental issue in all ideological disputation. For the incoherence of social-democratism derives from ambivalence about the way to answer the question: "Is it the business of politics to try to secure for people what they in fact want, or what they ought to want; what they think will be good for them, or what really will be good for them?" Political leaders with strong religious commitments, as well as those who have passionately espoused the secular creed of nationalism, together with both Marxian communists and classically educated European imperialists, who often thought of themselves as Platonic Philosopher-Kings, have been at one in holding that, obviously, it is the business of government to ensure that people live the best possible life of which human beings are capable. Historically, it has been the most commonly accepted view that all government, in this sense, must be authoritarian. The alternative view, however, is that it is the business of government only to *enable* people to live as well as it is possible for people to live. To the question, "Why only enable people to be good or happy when this can be ensured?" a powerful answer is that restricting government to the business of enabling people to live well is compatible with respecting the fact that people are free and autonomous agents. And that is itself, arguably, an indispensable condition for human beings to be either good or happy.

CHAPTER SEVEN

NATIONALISM AND INTERNATIONALISM

The story so far has focused on domestic politics, the internal politics of nation-states. But there is another element of communist theory, and the failure of Communism in practice, which is of equally crucial importance for an evaluation of the TOLD thesis and for any consideration of what beliefs and behaviours are likely to be prevalent in the post-Communist world which is presently emerging. This concerns international relations: how nation-states perceive and conduct themselves in respect of one another.

Of all Marx's predictions the most disastrously and decisively wrong was his belief that antagonism between nations would steadily diminish as the world's workers in different capitalist countries came increasingly to realise that what they have in common, as members of the international proletariat, runs deeper and is more important than what divides them as members of different nations. Marx and Engels thought that, as the power of the proletariat grew inexorably within capitalist countries, the hostility of nations towards one another would disappear. Nationalism is part of the ideological progeny spawned by capitalism to further the economic interests of the bourgeoisie and to conceal from the proletariat the true nature of its members' interests — and so the true identity of their real enemies and allies. But the reality is that the workers of the world everywhere have the same fundamental interests and belong to no nation or country in the bourgeois sense. They, therefore, have no need of the chauvinism and xenophobia which are are fostered by the ruling classes of capitalist nations as weapons in the war between internationally competing bourgeoisies.

Nationalism is part of the ideology which prevents the workers of the world from recognising that their real interests must be served by international class unity, rather than by participating in national and nationalist conflicts. With the disintegration of capitalism, the fraud, whereby workers were deceived into believing that they had a duty to their nation or country simply because, in some purely legal sense, it was theirs, would become increasingly exposed. When this happened the teachings of bourgeois nationalist ideologues would be rejected, and international working-class solidarity would transcend and replace national loyalty as the driving force of international relations. And this solidarity would be an irresistible force in the world, for peace rather than war.

In 1914, for a vast complex of reasons which remain disputed by historians, a ferocious war erupted and spread world-wide. But one fact remains indisputable. This is that the workers of the world in different capitalist nations did not unite but rather allied themselves overwhelmingly, and with passionate enthusiasm to the cause of making war on their national enemies and so on their fellow proletarians within those enemy nations. This war was characterised by a mixture of ferocity and futility on a far greater scale than anything that had been seen on earth before. Worse still, the terms of the Treaty of Versailles which concluded it were so wounding materially and psychologically for Germany that they prepared the political soil for the emergence of the deranged nationalism of Hitler's Nazism. These wounds were neither tended nor cauterised, but left to suppurate until eventually they exploded into the calamity of the Second World War. But even after the defeat of Germany, Italy and Japan, though Fascism was so discredited that hardly anybody can tell you nowadays what it really means[1], nationalism as a political creed continued to flourish.

In the industrialised countries, nationalism became soft-surfaced

---

1. The essence of Fascism is the assertion that individuals can only flourish as human beings to the extent that they learn heroically to subordinate their private interests to those of their "people" (*Volk*), nation and/or race, where these latter interests are conceived in terms not of material prosperity but of glory, especially military glory. It is a creed which is extremely hostile towards liberalism, which it

and took on the (as we shall see, deceptive) appearance of being innocuous. It expressed itself primarily in economic and cultural competition and was anti-imperialist and officially quite fiercely anti-racist. As such, it has facilitated the emergence in the countries of the Third World[2] of a nationalism which has been vigorously militant even, when as with Ghandi, its tactics were professedly non-violent. This nationalism, far more than communism or the versions of socialism with which, at the time of the "struggle for independence," it often entered into alliances of convenience, provided the ideological fuel which enabled the Asians and Africans to chase out their European rulers and motivated the North Vietnamese so intensely that they were able to encompass the military defeat of the United States.

One of the most obvious and immediate consequences of the collapse of the Soviet Union has been the recrudescence of many nationalisms in places where the claim to nationhood had been

equates with moral enfeeblement and democracy against which it sets populist dictatorship. It is thus authoritarian in that it demands absolute obedience to the Leader, *Fuehrer* or *Duce* or *Tenno* (Emperor); it is also totalitarian in that there is no aspect of the citizens' lives which the State does not have the right to control completely. Nationalism does not entail Fascism though it easily leads to it. This is because both begin from the premise: "My 'people' (however defined) are wrongly treated as inferiors." However, where the nationalist needs only go on to say: "But the reality is that we are the equal of other peoples and should be treated as such," the Fascist says: "But the reality is that we are superior to other peoples and should treat them accordingly."

2. Coinage of this phrase (originally *le tiers monde*) is attributed to A. Sauvy by the French journalist, G. Balaudier. Originally it referred to the twenty-nine countries which participated in the Bandung Conference in 1955. These were Afro-Asian countries, including China, which wished to disassociate themselves with both the Western and Eastern blocs as they were. The phrase now refers to "developing " countries, which are typically poor and without significant manufacturing industry. Their economic circumstances were until recently supposed to contrast both with the industrialised capitalist world and with the industrialised world of the Soviet Union and its allies. Similarity of economic conditions was thought to provide a basis for co-ordinated political action. Hence, the "Non-aligned movement." Although the idea of the "Third World" has lost literal significance with the disappearance of a recognisable "Second World," it is still useful as shorthand for referring to the countries of the world which are poor by comparison with the West.

long thought to be dead, at least by most Westerners. Azerbaijan, Armenia, Kazakhstan, Latvia, the Ukraine, Georgia — these are only some of the better-known nations to have asserted their nationhood within what used to be the Soviet Union. And in formerly Communist Eastern Europe, the fissile power of nationalism has shown itself in the dissolution of Czechoslovakia and in the bloody war of dismemberment in what was Yugoslavia. Here Croatians and Slovenes, but not the Bosnians, have sought and secured a tenuous national independence from Serbia. This once unproblematically multi-cultural society now seems destined to be devoured by its greedy neighbours, exploiting the discreditable morality of militant nationalism and physically extirpating and even exterminating the Muslims.

Given all this, it might be thought that it is nationalism, rather than liberal-democratism which has triumphed decisively in the wake of the fall of Communism. This thesis becomes more persuasive when one considers that the ideologies with which nationalism allies itself are typically matters of shallow convenience. Thus, where nationalism in the past, as for example in Egypt, found it convenient to ally itself with communism in the fight against imperialism, it also found it necessary to distance itself dramatically from communism once national independence had been achieved. Elsewhere nationalism has allied itself with a major religion, as in the Middle East and Northern Ireland. In the Third World the explicit self-designation of most of the countries concerned as "non-aligned" suggests flexible ideological allegiance, provided only that national sovereignty is respected and national interest served.

However, despite all the evidence of its past and present potency in the politics of the last two hundred years, it seems to me that, as an ideological force in global politics, nationalism is likely to become increasingly enfeebled now that Communism has collapsed. In brief, my argument is that, if an ideology is to remain powerful, it must be credible and if it is to be credible, it must be apparently coherent. In the case of nationalism, the ideology is not coherent and events are likely to make that incoherence so apparent that the doctrine will become discredited. I am not underestimating here the fact that nationalism in practice is more a matter of political passion and rhetoric than of theory and doctrine; and nationalist passions are likely to continue to be assiduously and often successfully inflamed by political leaders seeking to make a powerful impact on the emotions of their potential supporters. Nevertheless, nationalism does articulate political principles and it does prescribe specific political arrangements. If these turn out to be transparently indefensible from a moral point of view and/or unworkable in practice, the power of appeals to nationalist sentiment is bound to grow weaker.

By "nationalism" I understand the doctrine that those who belong to the same "nation" should be governed by their fellow nationals in a sovereign, independent state, in whose domestic affairs other national states have no right to intervene. This is the creed at whose heart lies the principle or doctrine of national self-determination which has fuelled struggles for national liberation for some two hundred years; which has been more or less officially recognised as authoritative in international relations at least since Woodrow Wilson; which is enshrined in the Charter of the United Nations and associated documents; and to which all member countries at least pay a pious sort of lip-service.

The view that the principle of national self-determination is in decline is one which requires to be supported by empirical evidence. But before proceeding to empirical matters, it is, as always, crucial to be clear about the meanings of the terms and the nature of the concepts under discussion. In particular, it is crucial, for present purposes, to be clear about what a "nation" is supposed to be and in what sense it might possibly be "self-determining".

Etymologically, "nation" refers solely to the group one is born into. In historical practice, however, nations have been defined, objectively in terms of positive law, as the group to whose jurisdiction one is subject by birth or "naturalisation." They have also been defined, subjectively, in terms of supposedly shared cultural, territorial and kinship affinities and affections. The national "self" in "national self-determination" is, thus, supposed to be an amalgam of these objective and subjective elements, so that those who feel that they belong to the same nation are also normally subject to the laws made by their "own" national government.

What must be noticed here is that, on both definitions, "nations" are literally fictions: that is, artefacts, in the first case, of man-made[3] law and, in the second, of man-made culture. One's nationality is thus different from, for example, one's gender in that it is not a matter of observable biological fact. These linguistic truths need not provoke the cynicism about nationalism implicit in the anonymous nineteenth century claim that "a nation is a group of people united by a common mistake about their ancestry and a common dislike of their neighbours." It should, however, encourage a healthily sceptical caution about claims that people have rights and duties solely in consequence of their "naturally" belonging to different "nations".

Bearing this in mind, we can now turn to the resurgence of nationalist parties, passions, politics and politicians in the erstwhile Communist world. The claim that these events do not, despite initial appearances, presage a successful revival of nationalist ideology rests on two main empirical considerations.

The first is that there are so many "nationalities" involved that they cannot all achieve independent statehood. In what is no longer the Soviet Union there are — depending on your authority and/or definition — some one or two hundred "nationalities". Moreover, the "republics" themselves, including Georgia, Kazakhstan and Russia itself, are ethnically mixed and their serious minority problems are likely to be exacerbated if independent statehood threatens to foster a resurgence of nationalism. For this reason, leaders confronting the formidable economic problems which were both cause and consequence of the collapse of Communism are likely to perceive fewer advantages and more and greater dangers than presently appear in the prolonged inflammation of nationalist passions.

The second consideration relates to what independence would

3. Only someone prepared falsely to claim that the making of laws generally and of those relating to nationality specifically has been equally the work of men and women would object to this use of "man-made" which here is gender-neutral and carries no implication as to the sex of the human-beings who did the law-making.

really be worth, even where it was achieved. On the one hand, there is already the question of nuclear weapons, which everyone agrees cannot be shared amongst self-determining national republics, each with their own nuclear weapons policy. Such a prospect is far too dangerous. On the other hand, the real independence of newly recognised states in the Balkans, for example, is likely to be seriously attenuated for economic reasons. Indeed the main reason for the independence of a state like Slovenia was not nationalist passion, but the hope of improving her prospects of getting into the European Community, which is a powerfully anti-nationalist phenomenon as we shall now see.

There is no question that membership of the European Community diminishes national sovereignty and this is a process which will increase in scope as the Community develops. (Despite current palpitations over Maastricht, it seems to me that convergence of economic, social and defence policy in Europe is inevitable.) Mrs Thatcher (as was) was (and is) right about this. Whether she is also right, to deplore any limiting of Britain's right to national self-determination is another matter. For better or worse, present and prospective members will have to be not only committed to competitive democracy and a market economy; they will also have to toe the Community line on defence, international trade, human rights, energy policy, the environment and so on, with respect to all sorts of issues which used to be decided independently by sovereign national governments. Above all, Europeans will find that closer cooperation, whether through Exchange Rates agreements or a common currency, means that much economic policy and therefore much foreign policy, will have to be decided by some centralised European governing body. This means a drastic dilution of sovereignty and national self-determination for the members of European nations; nations recognised at least since the end of the Napoleonic wars by the Congress of Vienna (1816); reinforced by the unifications of Germany and Italy in the nineteenth century; re-established after the Treaty of Versailles (1919) at the end of the First World War and after the Russian Revolution; and then again and much more implausibly at Yalta (1944) to deal with the aftermath of the Second World War and the emergence of a world dominated by two Super-powers. Consequently the British and French and Scandinavians and all the others are indeed going to be governed to a substantial degree by "foreigners."

To object to this, on the basis of some strong instinct or prejudice that it violates the semi-sacred character of nationhood, is to beg the question and to miss the central issue. For the central question is whether nationhood, understood in terms of the cultural and regional interests of historically established groups, will or will not be best promoted by maintaining the maximum degree of self-government for these groups. This is not obviously the case because, in general, highly autonomous governments are not necessarily very powerful and, in the case of Europe, the price of retaining a high degree of self-determination would be increased political impotence, as measured in terms of what national governments could actually determine. This is why the newly independent countries of Eastern Europe, like Croatia and Slovenia, and the Czech and Slovak Republics are extremely eager to become as full and as equal members as possible of whatever "Europe" turns out to be.

To be "anti-European" on the grounds that it will mean being governed by foreigners is irrational because it is based on an increasingly misleading and incoherent stereotype of what "national" government consists in and can accomplish. Similarly, to object to laws under which one lives simply because they have been made by "foreigners" is irrational. What is far from irrational is to object to a proliferation of laws, no matter by whom they are made. It is this tendency in Europe which warrants real scepticism — at least on the part of liberal democrats — about the consequences of greater unification, especially since the laws, thus proliferating are not made by people who are subject to effective democratic accountability. Instead they are made by managerial and bureaucratic elites presumed to possess a necessary but recondite technical expertise.

The general lesson about nationalism which emerges from current European debates, is to be found in the fact that the politicians of Europe have felt obliged to discuss Europe almost entirely in terms of national economic self-interest, very narrowly conceived. What seems certain, however, is that national economic selfishness will no longer provide a feasible principle on the basis of which international relations can be rationally conducted. This is not just because collective and chauvinistic avarice is morally ugly — though it certainly is. It is rather because, despite its apparent benignity (it is not overtly violent) this kind of economic nationalism tends towards the intensification of Hobbesian anarchy in international affairs, which could well prove as dangerous as the older, more explicitly martial forms of nationalism. At all events, the notion that all that politicians can, and should be concerned with in their international dealings are the short-term and parochially conceived economic interests of their own "peoples" is demonstrably false. The truth is that such an exclusive fundamental concern is not possible. The economic interests of different peoples are extremely difficult to disentangle and such national selfishness conflicts with a long-term, global and "enlightened" assessment of where the true interests of people and peoples lie.

For the time being in Europe, however, it seems unlikely that countries like Romania or Albania, which have little prospect of becoming economically successful in the near future, will be welcomed into the Community, however plausibly and passionately their appeal to geographical proximity or historical sentiment is argued. Indeed the European Community seems likely to develop a ruthless exclusivity of its own, in which the acceptance of East Germany back into the European fold would be seen for the unique and exceptional, and still not very happy, case that it was.

Nevertheless, in both Europe and the erstwhile Eastern bloc we are likely to see a move away from the principle of national self-determination. In the former case this is clear as more power is transferred from national to Community institutions. In the Eastern bloc the process is obscured because the system that is being moved away from used to be an imperial hegemony. But the degree of national autonomy which is realistically achievable, by peoples formerly subject to both authoritarian and totalitarian rule, is severely limited and is not going to result in a proliferation of successful nationalisms, each forming its own sovereign, independent, self-determining, state.

The Middle East provides different kinds of arguments for the view that the principle of national self-determination in its classic form is already unsustainable. The Lebanon has virtually no prospect of recovering its status as a genuine sovereign state. Israel's independence is illusory in the sense that if the USA ceased to supply Israel with money and munitions, the country would become bankrupt and undefendable. Whether this will happen or not depends on a number of imponderables including the long-term decline of American wealth and power, vulnerability of American politicians to Anti-Israel groups, the Israeli handling of the Palestinian question if it becomes increasingly clear that "land-for-peace" offers no real solution, and so on. However, even on the worst scenario, from the Israeli point of view, where the US withdrew economic aid and political and potential military support, it seems hard to conceive that Europe would not take up the role of guarantor of Israeli survival.

There is however more to nationalism as it applies to Israel than physical survival: in particular, there is national self-respect. What the Israeli case exhibits with painful explicitness is that in some circumstances, the principle of national self-determination, and the principle of political equality which is the essence of democracy, cannot be reconciled. The starkest of these circumstances is found when two peoples, both strongly imbued with nationalist ideals, lay claim to the same territory. Israelis may one day be forced to choose between being nationalists and being democrats.

But in the Middle East the really illuminating case is Iraq. Whatever else the 1991 war was about, it was not about the right of the Kuwaiti nation to be self-determining. (The Iraqis, incidentally, had a legitimate economic grievance against Kuwait, sufficient to constitute a plausible *casus belli* in the eyes of most "Western" voters and leaders, had they known about it, which they didn't and, mostly, still don't[4]). What the war ought to have been about — and what gave it its perceived international justification — was preventing a ruthless dictator from

4. This was that after, having, as they saw it, kept Kuwait and other "secularist" Arab states safe from Iranian fundamentalism by enduring the vast costs and casualties of a protracted war, the Kuwaitis then proceeded to demand crippling war-loan repayments once peace was re-established.

committing atrocities against his own people, as well as threaten-ing to commit such atrocities internationally, especially with bio-logical and chemical weapons. In other words the principle of humanity towards Saddam's Iraqi victims ought to have taken moral and political precedence over his appeal to the "principle of national self-determination". It did not. The result was that a large number of innocent Iraqis were killed and Saddam Hussein remains menacingly in power. In this sense, the Americans won a battle but lost the war. But Saddam's very success in invoking the principle of national self-determination will serve seriously to weaken the plausibility of the principle in other contexts.

The message, here, will increasingly be that there are some things which governments may not do "even" to their own peo-ple, because these things are recognised as so morally appalling that respect for the principle of national self-determination ought to be jettisoned without compunction. If more people had known about the slaughter of one third of its own population by the Kampuchean government in the seventies, or if they had known earlier what was going on in Somalia, or about recent events in Liberia, they would have had no compunction about approving the intervention of foreign forces to stop the domestic carnage. Knowledge of such atrocities is likely to become more vivid and widespread.

Paradoxically, the same lesson emerges from the otherwise very different Falklands-Malvinas war, which really was fought in defence of the principle of national self-determination. Thatcher's subsequent popularity and the democratisation of Argentina were consequences but not causes of the war. So for the matter of that was a brief resurgence of British jingoism. But the real lesson of this war was that it cost, and continues to cost a fortune of money quite adequate to induce the Falkland Islanders to relocate several times over. Also, the number of lives lost greatly exceeded the number of the Islanders whose right to self-determination was being defended. (The current cost of the "Fortress Falklands" policy is estimated at £160,000 per Falklander per annum.) In hindsight, too, it could have been a lot worse for Britain: however brilliant their military strategy and prowess, they still needed, and got, a good deal of luck.

Was the principle of national self-determination really worth defending at this kind of cost and risk? Was there, and is there really no other way of settling the dispute other than the British policy of "Fortress Falklands" and "Sovereignty is not negotiable?". The Falklands war, in short, contributed to the discrediting of the very principle for which it was fought, by providing a *reductio ad absurdum* of where it can lead.

The same lesson is to be learned from yet another perspective by considering the case of South Africa.

South Africa used to furnish the one case where the principle of national self-determination could be violated with the world's approval and encouragement. Now South Africa is seen to be moving, albeit haltingly, in the direction which the world desired. But if the white government appeared to move unambiguously backward, this would be widely accepted as a sufficient reason to redouble international efforts to make South Africa's future political arrangements what the world thinks they ought to be. Whether or not international pressure did indeed help to bring the South African National Party to abandon *apartheid,* the fact that *apartheid* has been officially abandoned in South Africa strongly reinforces the view that hostile actions, in violation of the principle of national self-determination, can be both effective and benign. But if intervention can be shown to be both successful and morally justifiable in this case, why not in others where governments do worse things to their own people than practise institutionalised racial discrimination?

All these considerations suggest to me that the trend in future global politics will be away from the principle of national self-determination and towards some new political morality which will be commonly, if selectively, enforced. It seems most likely that the new dominant political morality in international affairs, replacing "national self-determination" as an indicator of the politically sacrosanct, will indeed be that of democratic liberalism. The emphasis will be focused on an unashamed concern with what happens to individuals, rather than to the elites who increasingly monopolise power in increasingly heterogeneous and interdependent "nations."

This view seems to receive confirmation from the way the West has moved in its response to Yugoslavia. At first, an even-handed non-interventionism seemed both politically prudent and morally defensible. With the Bosnian debacle, this position became no longer tenable and the threat of armed assault on those perceived or exposed as aggressors and atrocity merchants became unavoidable. Somalia was slower to elicit moral outrage from Western public opinion. Otherwise she might already have been rescued from the devastations inflicted on her people by feuding warlords. However, as and when the quasi-nationalist fighting in Yugoslavia begins to be replicated in the erstwhile Soviet Union, especially if one or more of the inheritors of the Soviets' nuclear arsenal is involved, then the moral imperative to enforce peace will coincide with politically irresistible considerations of perceived self-interest.

It is plausible to predict that, in the future, governments will be less and less able to hide from their atrocious treatment of their own people by invoking the principle of national self-determination. Factors which suggest that this is the case include increased economic interdependence, the need to combat international terrorism, the power of television to generate moral outrage amongst democratic electorates, the increasing need to formulate common policies on trans-ideological issues like the environment, the drug trade, AIDS etc. and an emerging consensus about political morality.

But the desuetude of nationalism, no matter how welcome it may presently appear, should not obscure the fact that the doctrine once served a valuable political purpose in securing self-respect for the members of societies routinely humiliated by being made to feel humanly inferior by "foreigners". This was true at the dawn of modern nationalism in late eighteenth century Germany and is most notable in the writings of Herder. Herder's great contribution was to stress that national cultures are various in both their natures and their virtues. Germanic culture had its own distinctive excellences which were not to be thought any the less of simply because they were different to those of French culture. To ignore this was to make the mistake which underpinned the cultural superiority complex of the French of Herder's day and the corresponding inferiority complex of his fellow Germans.

The same dynamic was at work in all the national liberation movements of the Third World. Here a consummated nationalism proved the most effective salve for the profound humiliations which their imperial masters had inflicted on them and which derived from entrenched inequalities, experienced as intolerably unfair and destructive of all sense of human self-worth. Nevertheless, as an ideology, nationalism has always been philosophically incoherent because it accords reality to the illusion of nationhood and rests on the palpable paradox that "self-government is better than good government." In fact nationalism has overwhelmingly led to very bad government throughout its career and wherever it has flourished. Now, in addition to being morally pernicious, it is also politically impracticable.

It does indeed seem probable that the new world order will be predicated on the proposition that governments may not, with impunity and thanks to some supposedly sacred right of national self-determination, treat their own people as immorally as they please. Unfortunately, the demise of nationalism carries with it a considerable risk that the new international world order which seems likely to follow on the conclusion of the Cold War will be, in many respects, worse than the one it replaces.

To see why this is to be feared, imagine a world in which it was more or less agreed, whether explicitly or not, that what morality requires is that governments should respect the rights of those who are governed in accordance with the prescriptions of liberal-democratism. The arguments which seem so cogently to support the view that the domestic politics of all states should be conducted according to democratic principles, and that the only justification for government activity is to enable people to live as seems best to them, will also seem to support, with equal cogency, the view that these are the principles which should regulate relations between states.

In other words, if the principle of national self-determination does indeed become enfeebled, as I have suggested it will, there is likely to be a revival of the old "Enlightenment" (as well as the socialist) doctrine that there should be a world government. This is the central thesis of the internationalism which made the children of the European Enlightenment think of themselves as citizens of the world and caused the central organisation of pre-Soviet communism to be called the "International," which is also the name of the movement's (international) anthem.

What is notionally accepted in the United Nations Charter, namely that all nations are equal, is in practice nullified by the veto power which may be exercised by any of the five permanent members of the Security Council: USA, Russia, Britain, France and China. This sham from the point of view of international democracy is likely to become more obvious now that there is only one Super-power left in the world, one, moreover, which has severe problems of its own and strong, widespread and deep isolationist instincts. Indeed, the most obvious consequence of the collapse of the Soviet Union has been to eliminate the category, "Second World," thereby transforming global politics into an arena where there are are only the "Have" nations of the "First World" and the Have-Not nations of the "Third." In such a situation, sheer force of numbers makes it inconceivable that elected governments in rich nations will concede real democratic decision-making in world politics, since they will fear, almost certainly correctly, that this would have catastrophic consequences for their perceived vital, non-negotiable interests, the most obvious of which is to retain their prosperous way of life.

On the other hand the enormous disparity between rich and poor nations is going to make the poor nations, who are in an overwhelming majority, increasingly angry and bitter at what, to them, is a manifest injustice born of the selfishness and greed of the rich.

The problem is exacerbated by the fact that this division between rich and poor, internationally, is going to reflect, with uncomfortable closeness, the division of the world by lightness and darkness of skin-colour, to the extent that it may appear that the new international order will be based on a system of global *apartheid*. It is only a little too glib and fanciful to flesh out the analogy here more precisely, and place the Americans in the role of the Afrikaners, as the dominant military and governing group. The support for Ross Perot's presidential candidacy in 1992 and the electoral insignificance of the Gulf War and of foreign policy generally was already, perhaps, indicative of the intensity of the kind of mind-set, which would be uncompromisingly tough about America's willingness to spend money only, but then spend it ruthlessly on things American — American ideals as well as American interests.

The Europeans, on such a scenario, would find themselves in the role of South Africa's English-speakers, as the class which co-dominates commerce, thinks itself culturally superior and sub-sists in ambivalent symbiosis with the politically dominant Americans. There will also be a class of "Brown" peoples, locat-ed mainly in South East Asia, of whom the Japanese (like South Africa's Indian population) are presently the most prominent, but whose relatively undisputed economic supremacy in this area is likely to become diluted. These peoples will find themselves caught uneasily betwixt and between, still feeling themselves to some extent despised and discriminated against. At the same time they will aspire to and partially gain the benefits of hon-orary membership of the First World on the basis of merit and history, and because they do not constitute a threat they may one day prove useful allies.

Then there will be the poor, oppressed and disenfranchised mass-es of the Third World, the victims of starvation, disease, tyranny and war, both civil and with their neighbours. Their appalling plight will only be relieved, so their leaders will claim, (and some in the First World will guiltily or self-righteously, but not dishonestly, agree) if the citizens of the First World are prepared to make the huge material sacrifices which would be called for in an equitable redistribution of resources between all the peoples of the world. The voting majorities in the First World countries however, will ensure that no leader who might seriously contem-plate the adoption of such a policy is ever elected.

The mechanisms for implementing this global *apartheid* will include the United Nations, which will increasingly fall under the control of the Americans.This will be especially true in respect of whatever increased military powers it may be expected to to take in order to "keep" and "make" peace in the world. Europe will largely acquiesce in this, though it will no doubt place some rhetorical distance between itself and the

Americans. The problem of refugees, which is becoming increasingly alarming world-wide, will impact with especial awkwardness on Third-worldlings, including the new ones from the former Soviet Bloc attempting to gain access to Europe and America. Both Europe and America will be increasingly difficult places for outsiders to get into: only those who are rich, possessed of useful skills and politically reliable will be eligible to join. The international courts will continue to have some real independence, but will be circumvented if they pose any serious threat to First World interests. Meanwhile, the whole system will be justified with the argument that the Third World would be even worse off if it were not for the generosity of the rich nations, who are their benefactors. Disaster relief funds are not likely to become less frequently necessary and their contributions to these will reinforce the West's sense of its own moral decency. Moreover, the West will argue with the same plausibility as used to be used by *apartheid* South Africa that if the West is so immoral why do so many people want to settle there?

The other way of looking at this international scenario, which is also another way of looking at *apartheid*, is in terms of Marxian class conflict. On this view, the First World plays the role of Capitalist bourgeoisie and the Third World that of exploited proletariat. This way of looking at matters, first elaborated by Lenin in relation to imperialism, is more attractive than the *apartheid* model, in that it leaves out the element of racism. It does seem, in any case, likely that Marxism will continue to exercise considerable influence amongst intellectuals in poor countries in virtue of the explanation it offers for their poverty in terms of exploitation by rich countries.

The weakness of such a Marxian analysis, however, seems to me to be that relations between the First and Third World are not accurately characterised as those of exploitation. There is no reason to believe that America is rich because Africa is poor or that Africa would become richer if America became poorer. The bitterness which characterises some aspects of the relations between the First and Third Worlds and the moral concern which these relations rightly generate result from the severe disparities in access to resources and essentially the problem is one of too many people chasing too few goods. This classic problem is certainly exacerbated by the very high level of consumption which First World countries deem to be indispensable not only for their ordinarily prosperous members (cars, deep-freezes, VCRs, home computers etc.) but also for their indigent: most Westerners on "welfare" because of their poverty would expect, for example, to have access at least to a television and a fridge of their own. On the other hand, this problem cannot be solved, any more than can its South African version, by forced redistribution. Even if there were enough to go round, and assuming that seeking to enforce egalitarian redistribution globally would not do disastrous damage to production, the rich could be expected to fight by any means to preserve their relatively high standard of living and it seems inconceivable that they could be defeated by force.

What is by no means inconceivable, and indeed already shows signs of occurring, is that the First World will conclude that, on the whole, it would be better off if the Third World were considerably less populous. This would dispose electorates in the West to regard AIDS, famine, drought and internecine wars in the Third World as perhaps not such a bad thing. The fear, therefore, from a humanitarian point of view must be that the First World, far from continuing to "exploit" the Third World will increasingly tend just to write it off.

On a bleak view, then, a decline in nationalism in the wake of the collapse of Communism, and a division of the world into large blocs or conglommerations, political and economic will lead to a situation in which the world's wealthy minority will find itself in an increasingly false moral position, on the one hand championing what it takes to be universal human rights against Third World regimes which violate these; but, on the other, paying lip-service to the nationalist doctrine of non-interference in order to prevent the tenets of democratism from prevailing globally.

The key question which will bring all this tension into focus is: "Why should any member of the United Nations have a permanent seat on the Security Council with a right to veto any resolution which the General Assembly may pass?" That question really is uncomfortably similar to the question: "Why should black South Africans not be allowed the same voting rights as whites?" It is possible that the world's fascination with South African politics and the intense moral passions which they have aroused internationally reflect a mostly unconscious recognition that the world as a whole is on the brink of facing, macrocosmically, the extremely intractable problems which gave birth to *apartheid* in the first place.

As early as 1964, arguing that, despite appearances, it is a blessing that the world order continues to be governed in accordance with the principles of nationalism, Ernest Gellner wrote: "If a politically unified world were passing through the second, global phase of industrialisation, this united world might well come to resemble the present condition of South Africa." (Gellner. 1964: 178.)

My argument has been that, with the collapse of Communism[5], the "blessing" of nationalism, if that is indeed what it was, is evaporating. If so, amongst the grimmer phenomena we are likely to witness are savage, perhaps genocidal wars amongst Third World countries in desperate competition for scarce resources and an escalation in global terrorism/freedom fighting, with a serious risk that such fighting may sooner or later involve nuclear weapons. The response of the First World is likely to be a mixture of impotence and indifference, on the one hand, and anger and anxiety on the other. Either way, the commitment to liberalism and democracy is likely to come under intense strain if it does not crack completely.

These gloomy prognostications need to be taken seriously as regards the short-term future of the post-Communist world. However they cannot adequately anticipate a world order sustainable over the medium term, say, beyond the end of the millennium. This is because they leave out of account the future of the two giants, China and Russia itself.

---

5. Ironically, the collapse of Communism may have increased the likelihood of nuclear warfare occurring, though not of the Mutually Assured Destruction variety. This is mainly because, no matter how many nuclear devices are destroyed, it is not possible to destroy the knowledge of how to make them.

China is already shedding Communist economics and pressures for political liberalisation seem certain to follow. The now notorious events in Tiananmen Square, as seen on prime time TV, confirm the view that it is becoming increasingly difficult for rulers to appeal successfully to the principle of national self-determination and of non-interference in the domestic affairs of sovereign states while they are at the same time denying their subjects liberal and democratic rights. With the advent of new leaders the process of liberal-democratic reform in China is likely to accelerate with Western support, though this will have to be accomplished with due sensitivity to China's acute sense of national pride.

As to Russia, if the commitment to liberal democracy fails for economic reasons, the most frightening alternative is collapse into economic chaos followed by an alliance of near Fascists and reactionary Stalinists supported by the still formidable military. The West cannot afford to permit such a collapse, no matter how insular and isolationist its electors may become: they will have to pay to prevent the restoration of a hostile and ruthless dictatorship. In the case of Russia at least, the West will have to pay to prevent its otherwise inevitable decline into Third World status and to achieve its affiliation on increasingly equal terms with the liberal, democratic and above all prosperous First World.

The hope here must be that the huge political influence which China and Russia will continue to have in world affairs, in virtue of their size and despite the fact that they will be struggling for some time to extricate themselves from widespread and severe impoverishment, will subvert the ruthless economic nationalism which would otherwise be likely to prevail in the West. It will do this simply by making a narrow and unabashedly selfish pursuit of national economic self-interest counter-productive, as well as dangerous and incompatible with the collective self-respect which is a by no means negligible motive in determining the attitudes of Western electors. This is also a more optimistic prospect for the rest of the Third World since the bridging position which Russia and China will continue to hold between the First and Third Worlds will make for an international order in which there is considerable opportunity for social mobility. On this scenario, Russia and China between them may, ironically, succeed in leading the Third World not into an international communist utopia, but into a more messy but still tolerable liberal (or social-democratic) world order. Thus, as the Third World grows through and out of the early stages of industrialisation, it will also find ways of eliminating the worst consequences of grinding poverty and gruelling, soul-destroying work and generating a modest measure of economic security for most citizens.

I believe that a major factor in making such a scenario more likely are the intellectual resources of the version of democratic liberalism which has indeed, in my judgment, triumphed, at least in the ideological struggle with both communism and nationalism. At all events economic nationalism, no less than the political variety, looks, despite superficial current appearances, an increasingly difficult ideology to sustain. In both politics and economics, federal arrangements of one sort or another, in a whole host of different contexts, seem likely to provide both the stuff of, and an umbrella for future international negotiations. Federalisms seem likely to prosper while two circumstances persist. On the one hand, the sovereignty and self-determination of independent nation states, as approved by classical nationalism, is steadily withering away. On the other, an international world government as dreamed of by the children of the Enlightenment remains at best an impossible dream; at worst a possible nightmare.

CHAPTER EIGHT

THE FAILURES OF IDEOLOGY

We are now in a position to draw together the threads of these arguments about secular political ideologies and to reach some conclusions about whether, in the wake of the collapse of Communism, what we are likely to see, and what it is desirable that we should see, is the triumph of liberal democracy. Initially it would seem we have reached the wholly negative conclusion that not only is communism now discredited as an ideology, but so are its principal rivals: liberal-democratism and social-democratism at the level of domestic politics, and nationalism as the fundamental moral premise of international relations. Nor does the picture look less bleak if we consider the two remaining logical alternatives to secular ideology, namely the revival of religious ideology and the more or less conscious and enthusiastic repudiation of all ideology, both sacred and secular.

The attempt to find a religious alternative to both communist and capitalist materialism has been most conspicuous among, though by no means exclusive to Muslims. Radical dissatisfaction with the perceived godlessness of both the Capitalist West and the Communist East has been at the heart of the revival of what is misleadingly[1] called "Islamic Fundamentalism." From a political rather than a religious point of view, what has been important about this movement has been the enormous boost it has given to essentially nationalist passions. Hostility to the atheistical

---

1. "Misleading" because Islam is necessarily a "fundamentalist" creed: its central doctrine, apart from the assertion of monotheism, is that the Koran uniquely articulates the mind of God as communicated directly to his prophet Mohammed. It is therefore a quite different instance of Holy Scripture from either of the libraries which constitute the Old and New Testaments. In Islam, therefore, the question

communist tyranny of the Soviet Empire was as natural to Muslims as to Jews or Christians. But insidious forces, familiar from the history of nationalism, have also been at work since the period of decolonisation, fomenting potentially explosive hatred for the West and especially the United States. Thus a perceived lack of ability by most people to achieve parity, in materialistic terms, with Western standards of living has combined with a genuine distaste for the apparent immorality of modern Western culture to entrench a deep-seated aversion to "Westernisation". When, to this, is added the widespread resentment of nations who feel, or can be made by their leaders to feel, that they have been treated as second-class citizens of the world by an arrogant, ignorant and bullying United States and its satellites, it is easy to see why appeals to rediscover the values and virtues of a purifying, militant and emphatically non-Western faith should be so effective.

It does not follow, however, that the nationalist passions thus unleashed and nurtured have any substantial chance of prevailing in political practice over the "Satanic" West, as it is thought and spoken of by genuine fanatics. It does not even seem to be on the cards that Islamic fundamentalism will be able to generate much transnational unity within the Muslim world. What seems more likely is that the quasi-nationalist political passions which the revival of any religion can be used to generate will remain intense and will provide varying degrees of apparent legitimacy to campaigns of terrorism which will be very difficult and painful to deal with, but which will not seriously threaten the collapse of Western culture or power.

The real significance of the Islamic revival is — as no doubt it should be — religious, and as such it is to be connected with the more general disenchantment world-wide with a purely and often brutally secular culture. This disenchantment manifests itself partly in more or less dramatic revivalist movements in other religions, ranging from "charismatic" Christianity through ultra-

cannot arise of whether we are to take everything contained in the Koran as literally true: the only questions that can, and of course, do arise concern the correct interpretation of the text, not, for example whether large parts of it are to be read as mythology.

orthodox Judaism, to devotion to all manner of cults and sects, including Satanism. Also symptomatic is the multi-billion dollar industry in quasi-gnostic writing which purports to reveal the secrets of easy success in all departments of life, from making love and money to tapping intra-psychic and extra-terrestrial sources of alleged power. Less obvious, but more serious and significant, is the proliferating enthusiasm in the West for the facts and fictions of, especially, Jungian psychology, of mysticism and meditation, and of self-help groups of the "Alcoholics/Narcotics/Overeaters/Gamblers etc. Anonymous" variety. Here intensely practical "life" problems are addressed by a programme which is grounded in classical pastoral theology, mainly Christian, but also drawing on important aspects of Eastern religions.

What all this betokens is a hunger for things sacred and spiritual and supernatural, and a rejection of the kind of ideology in which human happiness is made wholly dependent on the unedifying and unenduring satisfactions of shopping. This itself has negative implications for the end-of-ideology thesis. For the popularity of these movements, all of which claim to be non-political, reflects a profound distaste for, and disillusionment with, what is thought of as "politics as such", but is really politics based on any of the available secular ideologies.

This makes the prospect that human-beings henceforth will increasingly go about their business free of all ideology implausible in the extreme. The real truth contained in the "end-of-ideology thesis" as originally developed and as now resurrected turns out to be very different to what its champions envisaged. Although ideological conflict between traditional Left and Right, between socialism and liberalism, between Communism and Capitalism, has dwindled, there is no sign that people have lost interest in ideological issues. On the contrary, large numbers of people in modern societies are ideologically famished. Certainly it is hard to resist the conclusion that, for many, the failure of Communism has been traumatic in precisely the manner of events which seem to compel the abandonment of a religious faith. Far from having settled down into a condition of broad agreement about matters of ultimate ends, where politics becomes a purely pragmatic and instrumental affair, people are hunting for authentic ideological fare which will be substantial, attractive and genuinely nourishing. They are seeking metaphysical foundations for principles of conduct which will not only give them purpose and power in their private lives, but which will also take the perceived squalor out of public life and recreate a place in politics for genuine moral inspiration.[2]

This hunger is likely to express itself, not in some kind of humanistic consensus, but in a resurgence of religious belief. This will be boosted by the quite dramatic move away from conventional atheism which seems to be occurring among natural scientists and, to a lesser extent, philosophers. How this will affect conventional religious belief will depend largely on the ability of the institutional Churches to minister to people's need for the sacred, the spiritual and the supernatural. This will involve a reappraisal of their present role in which they appear essentially (rather ineffectual) secular institutions in a world where purely secular culture is proving increasingly unsatisfying.

So this development is no cause for complacency, let alone triumphalism among the champions of traditional religion. It is certainly not obvious that a widespread recovery of religious belief would prove good for institutional religion in its presently familiar forms, whether we think of Christianity in the USA, of Judaism in Israel, of Hinduism in India or of Islam in and around the Middle East. It is also far from clear that a resurgence in demand for what is thought of as political idealism will lead to greater virtue, understood in terms of humaneness, in political practice.

Humane politics require, above all, an intelligent realism about mundane practical possibilities. They are actually threatened

2. By "metaphysical" I mean "concerning questions about ultimate realities" foremost amongst which are: "Why does the Universe exist?" "What is the nature of persons and of consciousness?" "Is there a God?" "Is life eternal?" "What are Goodness and Evil?" It is the lack of clear and convincing metaphysical foundations, that is of a theory about the nature, condition and destiny of ourselves and our universe, which makes liberalism seem (wrongly, as I proceed to argue) uninspiring and morally thin, if not downright desiccated — as both John Dunn and Robert Nozick, amongst others and in different ways, have noted.

when political life becomes dominated by the vain repetition of pious intentions accompanied by inflexibility on matters of principle of the sort expressed by Luther in his famous assertion: "Here I stand. I can do no other." For the martyr this may be genuine heroism, but it is rarely more than cynical tub-thumping on the lips of the practising politician. This is not to state a cynical view to the effect that morality has no place in politics: it is rather to stress that what morality requires in politics is to be measured in terms of concrete and specific results and not in either good intentions or noble general principles. For these reasons I conclude, on the one hand, that the promise of a new era, free of ideology, is turning out to be neither possible nor desirable: people cannot, do not and should not want to live lives voided of all moral and metaphysical conviction. On the other hand, the proposal to revive political arrangements supposedly based on the rediscovered truths of religion, as vouchsafed to a priestly elite, offers only the prospect of a return to a cruelly fanatical religious authoritarianism. Such supposedly theocratic politics have not only been rejected by secular humanists since the Enlightenment on the grounds of their inhumanity and irrationality: they are also demonstrably incoherent and self-contradictory on their own theological terms, since they deny both divine love and human freedom.[3]

I do not, however, think that the argument about the prospects for ideology after Communism need reach this kind of dead end. According to this view, all the principal ideologies available to us have gone bankrupt — including the traditional ideologies which were based either on religion or on the humanism of the Enlightenment as well as their their modern inheritors which dream either American or Marxian dreams, and all forms of contemporary nationalism and sectarianism. On such a scenario, the world's ideological future would be set to become increasingly irrational and chaotic, exposed on the one hand to the four horses of the apocalypse[4] in the Third World and to dehumanisation and moral degradation in the First. This is undoubtedly a clear and

3. For a fine elaboration of what's wrong with religious authoritarianism in politics from a religious point of view as well as a political one see Gordon Graham: *Politics and Religion*. (Philosophy. 1983).

4. War, famine, pestilence and death.

present danger which perhaps anticipates what is most likely to happen over what remains of this century. But no logical necessity requires such a pessimistic forecast, nor is it warranted by considerations of historical inevitability. More positively, it is not something about which the world is impotent. Specifically, we can, I believe, construct from both the past successes of liberal democratism and from its most serious failures, a version of this ideology such that, if it is clearly understood, it becomes rationally persuasive and attractive to modern sensibility. The claim here is that, in this version, liberal democratism offers accounts of the way we are and of the way the world is and could be which are credible in themselves and which indicate principles of political conduct capable of commanding intelligent assent and allegiance. As such it can be harnessed in the service precisely of averting the worst of what the future threatens.

Before expounding this version of liberal democracy, it will be useful to review the principal reasons for the apparent discrediting of the ideological doctrines we have considered so far. This will make plain what any post-Communist ideological position, whether liberal-democratic or not, will have to be able to answer and accommodate if it is to possess intellectual cogency, political effectiveness and moral authority.

The process whereby an ideology comes to be discredited intellectually is typically one where it is overtaken by events which it is unable to account for and which consequently expose incoherences within the ideology itself. But ideologies become more decisively discredited when, in moral and political practice, they fail to deliver on their promise to set us free from tyranny, in the struggle against which the pursuit of liberty and the pursuit of justice coincide. What we need to ask, therefore, in reviewing the present inadequacies of past ideologies is: "What is it about the modern world which they were unable to account and provide for?" Or to put the same point a little more sharply and the other way around: "What are the forms of tyranny under which we presently suffer and why have our political theories failed to set us free from them?"

In the case of the liberal part of liberal democratism, in its Enlightenment form, the most crucial discrediting event was the extreme misery — material, psychological and spiritual — generated by industrialisation. This has been the most powerful reason for causing people to think that, in the economic domain, where liberalism is identified (in part, wrongly) with what is often tautologically called "unbridled free enterprise" (itself wrongly taken to be synonymous with "capitalism"), the most obvious and deplorable consequence of prosecuting the cause of individual liberty is the creation of mass servitude. This servitude originally appeared as a function of the fact that, in large modern industrialising societies, most people's lives are so consumed with the struggle to eke out a bare subsistence that they have only the minutest scope for exercising freedom of choice.

This was certainly an accurate diagnosis of the situation in the early-to mid-nineteenth England which was Marx's primary target, and it still describes the condition of life for vast numbers of people in the Third World. In modern affluent societies, the tyrannical character of capitalism appears most perniciously in the ills associated with earning money and relating to other people and to the world about us, which Marx so brilliantly diagnosed, even though he was unable to prescribe an effective cure. These ills are reinforced by the susceptibility of most people to indoctrination through advertising which cruelly distorts their self-image, making them want to have and to be things which are neither possible nor desirable. Then there is the sterile and antagonistic character of their work, as well as the triviality of their leisure pursuits: having laboured as clerical helots in the soulless buildings where a few fat rats do their racing, they return to media-generated amusements in which the events of the real world are rendered indistinguishable from those of a violently titillating soap opera[5]. Intimate relationships, notably family life and friendships, shrivel. The idolatrous worship of other people's opinion transforms private creativity and public commitment into the merely modish. Concerns for art and for politics become merely roles, played at by people who would be thought artistically cultured and politically correct. And more generally in the modern worldliberal freedom seems in reality to make people prisoners of vanity, loneliness, status-hunger, repressed aggression, and/or unrequited self-love.

5. See on this Neil Postman's fine book with the excellent title: *Amusing Ourselves to Death*.

As a cure for the material and spiritual poverty of modern living, social-democratism, with its social markets, has fared no better than liberal democratism, with its capitalism blue in tooth and claw. As to the alleviation of the problems of the very poor, social-democratism appears to have resulted principally in a bloated, ruinously expensive, ineffective and unaccountable bureaucracy which has professionalised private charity and created a vested interest in keeping clienteles "helpless", numerous, powerless, dependent and pathetic. The related problems of inner-city decay — impoverished single-parent families, ethnic ghettoes and discrimination, unemployment, crime, delinquency, drugs and all the other ills associated with what is nowadays called the "Underclass" — all these seem alike immune to the policies of the "new Right" and the "old Left" in Europe and America. Not surprisingly, one of the most striking features of this Underclass is its members' conviction that all politicians, of the Left as well as of the Right, are profoundly ignorant of and indifferent to their real circumstances and interests.

Perhaps, however, a deeper weakness of the social-democrats' case has been their failure to address the spiritual impoverishment of modern life and to avoid the charge of being "Vulgar Marxists."[6] For there is one feature of human bondage in the modern world which is curable neither by increases in the availability of commodities, nor by greater evenness in their distribution. This may be called "the tyranny of consumer culture." The claim here is that social democrats tacitly accept the supposed premise of capitalism, that human happiness consists in maximising the accumulation of material things, and think that what socialism requires is the making available of happiness to the masses through the redistribution of wealth. This objection to

6. This phrase denotes at least part of what Marx meant when towards the end of his life he declared that, whatever else he was, he certainly wasn't a Marxist. Vulgar Marxism, roughly, refers to a combination of what "orthodox" Marxists perceive as a naive and aprioristic economic reductionism with an unrealistic reliance on the reform of morals and a simplistic utopianism. The phrase is parasitic on "Vulgar Economics" by which Marx meant Pre-Ricardian capitalist economics of the sort which believes capitalism's own self-justifying moral propaganda. See the letter from Engels to Conrad Schmidt of Aug 5, 1890.

social-democratism has been forcibly articulated by John H Schaar and lies at the root of the thought of neo-Marxist writers such as Herbert Marcuse and Erich Fromm. Schaar, thinking of himself as a Left-wing radical, writes of equality of opportunity, which he takes to be the dominant ideal of the North American Left, as follows: "it opens more and more doors for more and more people to contribute more and more energies toward the realization of a mass, bureaucratic, technological, privatized, materialistic, bored and thrill-seeking, consumption-oriented society — a society of well-fed, congenial and sybaritic monkeys surrounded by gadgets and pleasure-toys." The servitude of affluence may be no less servitude than that of poverty, and because it is more insidious and less visible, it may be harder to escape.

But if economic and cultural developments in modern societies, have seemed to render worthless, if not downright fraudulent, the claim to secure freedom for all individuals and all classes, the democratic component in both ideologies has also failed to provide the guarantees against government tyranny which has been its principal promise and justification. This is partly a matter of the manipulation of private choices in the economic and political spheres by advertising, propaganda and other forms of deceit, which make it difficult for people not only to express preferences, but to form them in the first place by thinking about them intelligently and independently. But the more pervasive and potent enemy of liberty under democracy has been bureaucracy in all its protean forms. For all Western democracies, liberal or socialist, have so far proved unable to remedy the situation whereby, although the people exercise power over their legally elected rulers, these elected officials themselves are largely impotent in respect of the unelected officials who form the permanent bureaucracy. Nor should it be thought that the problem of bureaucracy is confined to the overtly public sector of professional civil servants. The worlds of the large corporation, of financial institutions like banks and insurance companies, of Trades Unions, of medicine, of social work, of institutionalised religion, of education and many others have all increasingly become bureaucratised; that is dominated by people whose job is not to produce goods and services, to achieve specified results and solve particular problems, but rather to formulate and administer regulations. The result is a widespread and sickening sense that when confronted with these organisations and these professionals the ordinary individual is humiliatingly helpless.[7]

Such bureaucracies are elites of self-selecting and self-replicating professional experts. Their power derives from their expertise, real or presumed, but their primary interest lies, not in achieving success in whatever activity they are engaged in — producing goods, improving the circumstances of workers, the enhancing of health services, financial services, welfare, pastoral care and learning. Their principal interest is quite naturally the advancement of their own careers, and this requires that their principal talents be for "office politics" especially in the sense of being "good in committee" and behind the scenes of committees. There is nothing wrong with the ambitiousness of the manager, administrator or bureaucrat, nor necessarily anything intellectually or morally more to be despised about being a regulator than there is about many other lines of work. Indeed, as far as government is concerned, bureaucracies are typically composed of men and women who are not only not especially wicked or incompetent: they are often more principled and hard-working and, almost invariably, they are more expert in the business of governing than are the victors of electoral struggles. But

---

7. Hostility to bureaucracy and hence to all forms of government in the modern world has never been more forcefully expressed than by the nineteenth century anarchist Pierre-Joseph Proudhon who wrote: "To be GOVERNED is to be watched, inspected, spied upon, directed, law-driven, numbered, regulated, enrolled, indoctrinated, preached at, controlled, checked, estimated, valued, censured, commanded, by creatures who have neither the right nor the wisdom nor the virtue to do so. To be GOVERNED is to be at every operation, at every transaction noted, registered, counted, taxed, stamped, measured, numbered, assessed, licensed, authorised, admonished, prevented, forbidden, reformed, corrected, punished. It is, under pretext of public utility, and in the name of the general interest, to be placed under contribution, drilled, fleeced, exploited, monopolised, extorted from, squeezed, hoaxed, robbed; then, at the slightest resistance, the first word of complaint, to be repressed, fined, vilified, harassed, hunted down, abused, clubbed, disarmed, bound, throttled, imprisoned, judged, condemned, shot, deported, sacrificed, sold, betrayed ; and to crown all, mocked, ridiculed, derided, outraged, dishonoured. That is government; that is its justice; that is its morality." (Proudhon: 1923:293-4. Quoted in Nozick:1980:11.)

bureaucracies, national, sub-national and private, in modern democracies, do come to form a class above and apart from the populace at large and this class has distinct interests which are very often at variance with those of a majority of the people. Partly because of this, they have a strong interest in keeping themselves as far as possible immune from public opinion. Hence, amongst other things, their dangerous passion for "confidentiality" and their habit of representing deviousness as discretion. Above all they have a powerful interest, which they prosecute with considerable success, for frustrating what would otherwise be the natural operation of democracy, while all the while claiming to be its humble and obedient servants. Consequently, whether the public realises this or not, it is their powerlessness in the face of "Government," where government really means the bureaucracy rather than the legislature or the elected Executive, which accounts for current disenchantment with democracy in practice. Consequently, the principal challenge confronting modern democracies and modern democratic theory is how to ensure that the natural self-interest of bureaucrats is best served by giving the general public what it actually wants, with all the risks in terms of disorder and inefficiency which that is thought to entail. At present, there is a fundamental conflict between the requirements of liberal democracy and the interests of bureaucracies. Liberalism requires that there should be a minimum of official regulation of people's lives and that such regulations as there are should be clear and clearly necessary. This is also what democracy requires since it coincides with what most people want. This, however, is a desire which anyone whose business is the making and administering of regulations will have a powerful interest in frustrating because it inevitably means less employment and less power for administrators.[8]

In this connection, it should be emphasised that there is another group of people who have an even stronger and more insidious interest in the proliferation of legislation and regulation than

8. It is of some interest that this extremely serious point about modern government is only widely taken when it is made satirically, for example in the justly famous *Parkinson's Law* which is as profound a piece of social science as it is a witty one. The long-running British television series *Yes, Minister* and *Yes, Prime Minister* constituted simply a vast and very funny set of variations on this single theme.

legislators or civil servants. These are members of the legal profession: lawyers are technically bureaucrats, bound theoretically by codes of ethics, in that they are all "servants of the court", but their private practices also furnish them with a formidable pecuniary interest in promoting legal disputation which in practice works both against the interest of individual clients and of the ideal of justice itself. In America, in particular, liberalism is seriously imperilled by the explosion of litigative possibilities which the legal profession has succeeded in generating and which threatens to make of America a society governed not under the Rule of Law but under the rule of lawyers.

To sum up the argument thus far concerning the future of ideology after Communism, I am claiming that Marxist communism has indeed been discredited in terms of the prognoses and prescriptions it offered for life after, and without the miseries of industrial capitalism. But Marx's diagnosis of the evils of modern, secular, capitalist and professedly, democratic society remain both devastating and apparently unrebuttable. Nor will the social-democratic compromise come to our rescue and provide us with the principles we need to make sense of, and give meaning to our communal as well as our personal lives. Precisely because it is a compromise, social-democratism can neither address what is most profound in the Marxist critique of capitalism, namely the analysis/diagnosis of its effects on human personality and human relations, nor preserve what is most precious in classical liberalism, namely its refutation of the case for tyranny in any of its forms including the most benign.

On the other hand, this exposure of the fundamentally flawed character of the principal political ideologies which have competed for our allegiance over the last hundred years has not led, and is not likely to lead, to a kind of de-ideologised society where politics is solely a matter of horse-trading about interests and policies in pursuit of an agreed range of mundane goals and principles, as envisaged by the end-of-ideology thesis. If anything the denizens of the contemporary Western world seem to suffer from ideological bulimia, which compels them to swallow all manner of rich ideological stories but renders them incapable of retaining nourishment from any of them.

What seems more likely than the end-of-ideology scenario (although still not very likely) is that we shall see increasingly successful pressure for a religiously re-ideologised politics, which will re-legitimate the kind of moral authoritarianism and intolerance against which liberals have been struggling for three hundred years, and which is not only usually cruel but also intellectually incoherent in its own terms. Moreover, the ideological future of the West will be unfolding, I have argued, in a world in which the nationalist ideal, which claims that all nations have an equal right to self-determination, is becoming increasingly unviable. Nationalist passions will continue to fester and to flare up periodically, especially those of anger and resentment. For this reason it will remain useful for politicians to retain the fiction of commitment to nationalist principles and to accord them the kind of attenuated substance which can be accommodated within tolerance for, and even enthusiasm about "ethnic" and "cultural" diversity. But the reality will be a world which is increasingly unified in its economic aspirations and increasingly divided with respect to the ability of its peoples to satisfy those aspirations.

CHAPTER NINE

THE TRIUMPH OF LIBERAL DEMOCRACY?

From this survey it emerges that there are four main and radical weaknesses which continue to characterise all the ideologies we have considered. These are, first, the persistence of poverty and of the social tragedies which it engenders; second, the real powerlessness of individuals vis-a-vis the large institutions which dominate their lives and of which the largest is government itself; third, the inability to control world-wide the incidence of war, tyranny and destitution and so to provide for the problems of international society and of the planet as whole; and fourth, the failure to supply the majority of ordinary men and women with a unifying and inspiring vision of the world and of their place in it — a vision, whether, religious or secular, which will furnish them with a profound sense of the significance, purpose and dignity of human life.

The version of liberal-democratism which I believe could and should finally triumph with the fall of Communism is not new. It is explicitly championed in all the writings — about history and culture as well as about philosophy and politics — of Isaiah Berlin. The core of this doctrine also lies close to the heart of the ideological position of such otherwise very different political theorists as Karl Popper, Friedrich Hayek, Michael Oakeshott, George Orwell, the early Jean-Paul Sartre, Albert Camus and more recently of Giovanni Sartori, Stuart Hampshire, John Rawls, Robert Nozick, Bernard Williams and Ronald Dworkin amongst numerous others.

At first sight it seems highly implausible to suggest that these various thinkers share fundamental ideological convictions, or even that they can be said, without contrivance and distortion, to subscribe to a coherent ideological creed at all. However, this implausibility becomes substantially dissipated when we realise two things. First, that what they all have in common is a scepticism about the belief systems to which the various forms of mass barbarity and brutality which have so hideously disfigured twentieth century political history have owed allegiance. Secondly and less obviously, this shared sceptical disenchantment imposes on each of them the same keenly-felt obligation to provide security for such values as decency, humanity, integrity, compassion, courage, love, loyalty and friendship in a world where our only choice seems to be between some form of moral nihilism and some form of moral despotism, whether the despot be a Fascist or a Communist, whether claiming the authority of God or of History or of Reason.

The scepticism about the claims of authority, with which liberalism was born, has been forcibly separated by the history of the twentieth century from that confident optimism in the power of reason to solve all humanity's ills which suffused the democratic liberalism of the Enlightenment and which was bequeathed both to social-democratism and to Marxism. Contemporary liberal democrats are consequently most conspicuously united in what they are against. Thus, they are profoundly anti-utopian and anti-historicist: they do not believe that we are progressing, however haltingly, towards any kind of Promised Land, whether it be a Kingdom of Heaven upon Earth, a Utilitarian paradise in which pleasures are maximised and pains eliminated, a classless society of creative workers whose bonds of mutual affection will make government otiose, or a glorious empire of Super-beings that will last for a thousand years. Moreover, they believe that doctrines about the historical inevitability of attaining utopia are not only demonstrably false; they are also highly dangerous, because they authorise the violent abolition by the State of the rights of individuals in the name of the greater good of the collectivity, be it class, nation or Church.

On the other hand, modern liberal-democratism is emphatically not irrationalist. It does not prefer intuition, instinct, mystical insight or conventional wisdom to the conjunction of argument and evidence as a means of ascertaining the truth about the way the world is, about the way it could and should be and about what we ought to be doing about it. In both science and politics, modern liberal democratism retains a strong commitment to empiricism and pragmatism. In combination with a disposition to scepticism, this leads to an acute concern with what can go wrong in both theory and practice. This is most clearly seen in Popper's defence of the claim that a good theory is one which, above all, resists attempts to show that it is false, and a good policy is one which minimises harm while anticipating and making provision for the unintended consequences of the best-intentioned endeavours.

However, the scepticism which characterises modern liberal democratic theory is allied to a firm rejection of moral relativism and subjectivism, to the extent that these doctrines reduce all convictions about values to mere matters of opinion. Modern democratic liberalism espouses instead the thesis of value-pluralism. This is the thesis that in Isaiah Berlin's terminology, there are a number of "ultimate," "absolute" and "incommensurable" values, each of which can, from a moral point of view, properly constitute an end for individual or collective conduct, but each of which may also clash irreconcilably with others . Where such conflicts occur, we are confronted with a situation about which Berlin writes as follows: "Where ultimate values are irreconcilable clear-cut solutions cannot, in principle, be found," [consequently] "to decide rationally in such a situation is to decide in the light of general ideals, the overall pattern of life pursued by a man or a group or a society." (Berlin. 1969:l.) Where relativists and subjectivists claim respectively that values are idiosyncratic to a greater or lesser number of collectivities and individuals, for pluralists values are "ends in themselves" which are "presupposed (if that is the correct logical relation) by the very notions of morality and humanity as such". (1969. liii.)

Thus relativism and subjectivism deprive values of their "ultimate" or "absolute" character and consequently of their authority. Politically, they may lead to a tolerance born merely of complaisant indifference, but there is no logical warrant for this, since the values of a fanatical individual or society are no more or less valid than their opposite. Pluralism, by contrast, does provide solid philosophical security for the virtue of tolerance in politics, because the values it enshrines, as adopted by those who choose differently from ourselves, are not only not inferior to those that we choose for ourselves; they also have their own moral legitimacy and authority which we can recognise, even though we have chosen to give our own allegiance to different values. Subjectivism and relativism, find widespread acceptability not only amongst the young, to whose relatively unreflective moral generosity they appeal, but also and much more perniciously amongst theorists of "modernity" like deconstructionists. But ultimately they issue in a moral nihilism which denies the reality and the authority of any values whatsoever.

Amongst the values which Berlin (1969:xlix-l) cites as ultimate ends are "democracy, individual freedom, equality, artistic achievement, mercy, justice, spontaneity, efficiency, happiness, loyalty, innocence, knowledge, truth". To deny any of them is to be morally mistaken for it is not simply a "matter of opinion," of personal taste, inclination or preference whether, say, justice is or is not a morally admirable quality which can rightly be enjoined universally. On the other hand, justice may well, in real life, prescribe a course of action which is in conflict with what, say, liberty or mercy demand. And when such conflicts arise, they are irresolvable by appeal to some higher, over-arching principle. Pluralists thus reject monism, not because, like the subjectivist or relativist, they believe there are no absolute or ultimate values, but because, on the contrary, they believe there are many such values.

When pluralism is combined with a sceptical empiricism, it suggests the key to how liberal democrats might convincingly respond to the challenges of poverty, bureaucratic tyranny and international disorder, which, as we have seen, constitute the principal charges levelled against their doctrine. That these phenomena constitute evils is not in dispute: what is disputed are empirical questions about what policies will, in practice, mitigate these evils without the unacceptable sacrifice of other agreed values. This in turn will typically also require the careful philosophical elucidation of the meaning of terms. But to the extent that this is so, it follows that what are presently represented as ideological disputes about issues of principle are in reality most often disputes about the best method of analysing and resolving a particular concrete and practical problem. These are empirical and conceptual matters and, when recognised as such, they strip political disagreements of much of their confused, intractable and acrimonious character. This is the true and benign aspect of the end-of-ideology thesis.

For example, with respect to the problem of poverty, there is no dispute as to whether the relatively fortunate should be compelled, through taxation, to furnish some material relief to the very unfortunate. No-one seriously objects to the provision out of taxes of medical care for orphans. In general, it is not controversial that societies should, through what amounts to some form of compulsory insurance, provide a safety net to protect their members from calamitous misfortune. Disputes arise over the question of how this safety net should be constructed, how tight should be its mesh and how high it should be located. But these are questions about how resources can best be deployed so as to protect everyone from disaster and supply the basic welfare needs of those who are unable to do this for themselves. The desirability of these goals is not in dispute. What has to be argued over is the best way of securing them, while at the same time doing justice to other, potentially conflicting goals which are also recognised as desirable. In this particular case, the principal dispute is about whether the emergence of relatively large disparities in people's spending-power should be forcibly adjusted in order to mitigate the evils of poverty. Here, what is at issue is the extent to which the reduction of inequality will indeed lead to an alleviation rather than to an exacerbation of the evils of poverty, and how harmful such redistribution is likely to be in practice with respect to people's freedom of choice.

That poverty is undesirable and liberty desirable is not seriously in dispute. On the other hand, a little reflection on the meaning of terms indicates that the mere fact of differences in people's material wealth cannot reasonably be thought undesirable, unless these are also thought to be either, for example, psychologically harmful and/or the cause or consequence of injustice. We should not be deterred from accepting this by the fact that the issue is not typically presented as either an empirical question, or a conceptual one about the meaning of terms. Both professional politicians and their constituents have a vested interest in disguising how little they and their opponents disagree on matters of principle, for in doing so they conceal the extent to which conflict between them is really about naked self-interest. However, a principle such as Rawls's, to the effect that inequalities must advantage the least advantaged, can be readily accepted by a free marketeer like Hayek, who claims that in fact everyone, including the very poor, benefit when government refuses to use its coercive powers to limit economic inequalities. Who is right in this argument about free markets is a matter for empirical investigation: it is not or ought not to be construed as an issue of ideological principle.

These considerations apply even more plainly to the problem of bureaucracy in the modern world. No-one disputes that in areas such as education, health-care, social work etc. services of the highest cost-effective quality ought to be provided. There is also agreement about the desirability of minimal control over individual choices and maximum participation in the construction of regulations governing collective welfare in accordance with the principles of liberal-democratism. What is, however, vigorously disputed is whether in fact these goals are most effectively achieved by making the provision of the relevant services the responsibility of professionals employed by government and paid for out of taxation. *Prima facie* there would seem to be good reason for thinking that welfare is not best provided by career bureaucrats, whether professional welfare-providers or their government-employed administrators. This is not because the personnel who staff bureaucracies are necessarily incompetent, but they are typically inefficient because efficiency does not pay them. No-one denies that government requires efficient administration, as do institutions such as hospitals, universities and armies. Modern bureaucracies, however, are typically inefficient because bureaucrats have a strong interest in sustaining inefficiency. Thus, it is not in their interest to keep their administrations lean and inexpensive by employing as few professionals as possible and as cheaply as possible. Hence their hostility to freedom of choice in the provision of welfare, as manifested in their suppression of the competition which genuine deregulation of the welfare professions would generate. Hence also their hostility to competition from private charity.

The single example of educational provision suffices to demonstrate how issues concerning welfare, which appear to be ideological, in reality turn out to be about conflicts of interests, in this case the interests of professionals over and against those of the recipients of educational services and of society as a whole. The same arguments can be applied to the provision of healthcare, housing, food, social services and any of the other activities which have, since industrialisation, moved from the domain of private charity to that of state responsibility.

In the case of educational provision it is alleged that if education were not managed by the state, children would get a worse schooling than they could and should. There may, of course, be genuine disagreements between parties about the nature and particularly about the nuances of what constitutes a good education. But much the most important part of the battle over the bureaucratisation of education is not fought, at least openly, on ideological grounds. There is overwhelming agreement about the principles involved, such as that everyone should have access to as much education as they can profit from consistent with what society can afford; that education should not become a vehicle for indoctrination; that education should help to make people employable and able to function as citizens; that education should be diverse enough to meet the diversity of needs and wishes of the population to be educated etc..

The crucial question is whether these and other educational aims are best achieved by placing the control of education in the hands of professional civil servants and their political masters. It is significant in this respect that one proposal to meet what is agreed by all to be the poor condition of public education in the United States and Britain, namely restricting the state's responsibility for education to its funding and forbidding state control of the management and content of education, is advocated with equal vigour by radicals on the Left such as Ivan Illich and allegedly "far-Right" conservatives like Milton Friedman. It is also the position defended most eloquently in the concluding chapter of perhaps the most influential of all defences of modern liberalism, J.S.Mill's *On Liberty*. (1859:1910: 159-163.) It is disliked only by the monopolistic educational establishment, which of course stands to lose in terms of power, prestige and lucrative jobs. If such problems are to be solved, then clearly the question of vested interests has to be addressed and that is a problem which will require the deployment of considerable political skills. However, misrepresenting the problem as an issue of profound moral and ideological principle serves only to keep it out of the domain of the soluble.

The other way in which the professionalisation and bureaucratisation of welfare keeps soluble problems insoluble is by making their solutions prohibitively expensive. Not only must everyone be entitled, out of taxation, to the very best that professionals can provide, but all welfare problems are assumed to be soluble only if more money is spent on the service by the government. These two untenable views have brought the provision of public health-care to its knees in the United States and Britain by allowing the notion of entitlement to become completely divorced from affordability and creating a political climate in which all solutions which are cheap, in the sense of inexpensive, are vulnerable to the politically damaging charge that they are also cheap in the sense of being inferior.

Professional welfare providers have a collusive interest with their administrators precisely in keeping their problems grave and their solutions expensive. But this does not only apply in the public sector. Consider wage negotiations. Viewed dispassionately, it is not difficult to see that in the overwhelming majority of cases, the gap between what the company can afford and what the employees will accept is small and may be easily bridged. However, two groups of people have a clear vested interest in having frequent and lengthy wage disputes: the trades union negotiators and those who negotiate on behalf of management. The interest of union officials is transparent, that of management negotiators is better disguised. But it is obvious that in any organisation, those responsible for negotiating wages and averting strikes have a powerful interest in making those negotiations as difficult as possible and intensifying the threat of strikes because in this way the value of their role as trouble-shooters is enhanced: trouble-shooters have a vested interest in seeing that the supply of trouble which needs to be shot remains abundant.

Turning now to the sphere of international relations, we should note that where liberal democrats in the nineteenth century were romantically pro-nationalist, in this century they have been and remain predominantly anti-nationalist. This does not mean they are necessarily scornful of the patriotic affections and affinities which derive from a sense of shared identity amongst the members of ethnic groups. However, this is a matter of recognising certain psychological facts about the benefits which may derive from the sense of belonging to a group and the damage which often results when such a sense is absent. Otherwise liberal democratism is uncompromisingly universalist and individualist. It is because individuals everywhere are alike in being unique centres of consciousness — sentient, reflective and capable of choice — that they possess the same rights to be governed according to the principles of liberal democracy. To deny this in the name of national and cultural differences is the cant and chicanery of tyrants.

Unfortunately, as we have seen, liberal democrats cannot live up to their principles at the level of international relations. For the foreseeable future the perception will persist that political equality at the global level would conflict irreconcilably with the vital material and psychological interests of the world's richest and most powerful societies. As a result there will be considerable constraints on how far a commitment to liberal democracy can be permitted even in countries which pride themselves on their commitment to this system and these values. However, against this gloomy outlook must be set the consideration that international co-operation is going to have to increase in many areas where the interests of rich and poor countries coincide, with the result that a perception of global interdependence is likely to increase. These range from the economic to the environmental and include issues of crime, security and disease. What is more the ethic of liberal democratism itself generates an abhorrence of large-scale visible misery, which becomes a matter of public interest in its own right and cannot be ignored by democratic politicians. Democracy makes it harder to practise a wholly conscienceless politics in international as well as domestic affairs. To some extent United Nations involvement in ex-Yugoslavia, in Somalia, in Kampuchea, in South Africa as well as in the Middle East has been a function of moral concern within the electorates of the liberal democracies. Such a moral consensus, if and as it intensifies, is likely to lead to the emergence of informal quasi-federal international arrangements at the global level, combined, as federal arrangements typically are, with devolution to smaller-than-national regional units.

The question of the moral power of democratic liberalism brings us finally to the question of how far we are dealing here with a coherent ideology at all and, if we are, whether it is an ideology which is capable of furnishing adequate inspiration for individual and collective conduct in the post-Communist world.

The principal reason for thinking liberal-democratism a rather anaemic and lacklustre creed is in fact the strongest reason for accounting its vision of the human condition authentically heroic. This is its refusal to specify utopia as a desirable, let alone an inevitable destiny for human kind. This is much clearer in the version popularised by the French Existentialists of the immediate post-war period. Here the fundamental fact about the human condition is the inescapability of choice in a universe destined only to become what we make of it. Here there is no external source, justifier or guarantor of values beyond ourselves, such as God or Progress or Reason, such that our choice is restricted to obedience or disobedience in the face of irresistible power. In such a universe life can only be given meaning by an acknowledgment of our common humanity, which may express itself in shared sensuality, in friendship and a sense of human solidarity or in heroic resistance to the forces of a violent nihilism as incarnated in Nazism.

Though less dramatically stated, this emphasis on the centrality of freedom for an understanding of what we are is common to all modern liberal writers. From it follows inexorably that, as far as politics is concerned, the business of government is confined to creating the circumstances which make it possible for us to exercise our freedom of choice, and does not extend to determining what choices we shall actually make.

This profound account of men and women as autonomous moral agents, whose capacity for dignity derives precisely from the fact that they possess free will, yields the crucial claim that the most powerful and persuasive argument for liberal politics is a moral one. For a government which is "neutral between conceptions of the good life" (Dworkin:1978;127.), which is not "perfectionist" (Rawls: 1972: 332.) in that it prescribes one way of life as excellent or more worthy than any others, which, in short, seeks to maximise the scope for the exercise of individual choice, is the only kind of government which does not permanently infantilise its subjects and instead accords them the right to choose for themselves how to live, even at the risk that they will choose very badly. This freedom "is a curse but that curse is the unique source of the nobility of man.". (Sartre: 1954: 157.). And a politics which acknowledges and protects that freedom is the only kind which "would not affront their (human beings') autonomy". (Oakeshott:1976:366.)

There is some perhaps necessary tension in the value-pluralist liberal's conception of what should constitute the proper object of personal and communal endeavour, in that there exists a diversity of good and legitimate objects of human striving and in consequence of morally legitimate choices. But clearly not just anything goes, for that would return us to a condition of ethical anarchy tantamount to nihilism. What seems to bind together the liberal democrats' diverse conceptions of what ultimately makes life worth living is some fundamental conception of "humanity" as opposed to "inhumanity." It is in this sense that Sartre describes Existentialism as a "Humanism" and Berlin speaks of the "very notions of morality and humanity." A characteristic and attractive account of the ideological vision of modern liberal-democratism is to be found in an essay by the late British Labour Peeress, Barbara Wootton.

She writes: "This, then, is how the macrocosm and the human microcosm appear to one for whom supernatural interpretations have no validity. Such a view in an earlier generation was often labelled "rationalist"; and contrasts were often drawn between "reason" and "emotion", purporting to show that a "rationalist" philosophy must be cold, bleak and arid. Any such inference is wholly misconceived. Reason and emotion are complementary to each other, not mutually exclusive. The freshness of the dawn, the evening sunlight on the pine-trunks, the passionate love of man for woman and of woman for man, the deep satisfactions of parenthood and of artistic creation, the laughter of friends, the varieties and absurdities of animal life, even the daily pleasure of trivial things — these are what give warmth and colour and gaiety to agnostic lives as much as to any others. None of this has anything to do with the claim to divinity of a preacher who was shamefully put to death nearly 2,000 years ago; and the intensity of these joys is not dimmed if they appear to come and go in the brief flash that illumines the interval between birth and death." (In Ayer *et al.*:1966:218.)

This agnostic metaphysic, however, is not the only one that can support democratic liberalism. Such support also flows from forms of theism which emphasise that all human beings are equally special because all are made in the image of God and uniquely loved by their Creator. Their sojourn on earth is to be understood as a pilgrimage, or a saga, filled with adventures whose significance is spiritual and whose purpose is given in the possibility of free response to supernatural love.

I conclude, therefore, on the question of the ideological coherence and moral attractiveness of a liberal democratic world-view as follows. There are, as Isaiah Berlin himself often intimates, two broad classes of world-view, which are closely related to those elaborated in his justly famous essay; "The Hedgehog and the Fox." (Berlin: 1978: 22-81.) Both, at their best, are attractive and admirable but they are also mutually exclusive. The first is Berlin's and that of the majority of modern liberals who are religious agnostics. It offers a picture of the human condition which is at once genuinely tragic and genuinely cheerful. In ethics, it issues from, and in a deep appreciation of the rich variety of human goodness, of the many quite different ways of living which rightly command our admiration, of the diversity of worthy human aspirations and achievements and of the attractiveness of different understandings of the world and of ourselves within it. At the same time, this world-view is fully cognisant of the depth of man's capacity for inhumanity and of the many indifferent cruelties endemic in the universe we inhabit. This is because it is a vision which comes naturally to people who strive to be honest in seeing things as they are, at their most straightforward, and are consequently distrustful of stories about transcendent realities, said to lie behind or beneath the mask of appearance and ordinary experience, especially when such stories deny the tragic character of our mortality or of the real and difficult moral choices which we have to make for ourselves unaided by the "authority" of any creed which offers us pat answers. Above all, perhaps, this is a view of the world which is uncompromisingly secular and eschews all eschatology. It does not, however, normally embrace a militantly atheist creed, for it is respectful of the convictions of religious believers. It is, rather, pagan in outlook but in the tolerant manner of the ancient Romans, benignly disposed towards polytheism and feeling, with justification, seriously threatened only by a proselytising and exclusive monotheism. It is, in short, the world-view of Berlin's fox who knows many things, as against all manner of systems-building hedgehogs who know one big thing. And for all these reasons it accepts, defends and celebrates the pluralism of values and the liberal and democratic politics of tolerance, diversity and respect for autonomy which it underpins.

The other kind of world-view is first and finally religious, even when, as in Marxism, it repudiates religion. All its perceptions of the world are mediated through its vision of the ultimate end of the universe and of the creatures who inhabit it, whether these are the creatures of Platonic sunshine, of Nature, of progressive Historical forces or of a radically personal God. It is the "last things", which are hidden from ordinary and unaided common sense, that generate the elaborate and harmonious moral architecture within which we all live and with reference to which all decisions between right and wrong, good and evil, may be authoritatively settled. In consequence its ethics are essentially monist because they do not admit of the possibility of irreconcilable conflict and because all human lives are to be judged against one and the same *summum bonum*. It is a view which, in the end has no place for tragedy, since even where the end is conceived of in terms of personal extinction, "All things shall be well, and all shall be well, and all manner of things shall be well." (Julian, 1966: 103.) But this view too, in emphasising the virtues of charitableness, humility and the need to honour all human beings as creatures sublimely endowed by God with freedom of will, also requires the kind of politics which cherishes liberal ideals and democratic practices.

I think the case against the agnostic Fox's world view is that it is too bad to be true. The case against the eschatological Hedgehogs is that their view is too good to be true. I think we are all in different moods and moments attracted and repelled by both views. Moreover, both views have been corrupted so as to licence viciously illiberal political theories; the realism of the former being misconstrued to vindicate variations on the theme that might alone makes right; the idealism of the latter to justify fanatics in trying to impose their opinions on their fellows by force. How to adjudicate between these two world-views, when each is at its most clear and compelling is, in part at least, a mystery. But this should not be allowed to obscure the fact that both views, properly understood, support the contention that the only kind of politics which can be rationally defended is liberal democratic politics, because only liberalism and democracy do justice to an understanding of persons as first and foremost beings who make choices, and who must endure or enjoy the consequences. This is not a recipe for maximising human happiness, but it is a necessary condition if political arrangements are to respect the realities of human circumstances and to do justice to the essential source of human dignity which is grounded in our freedom to choose as morally responsible agents. In this sense it is true that, in as far as History becomes rational it will indeed steadily, if unspectacularly, tend to culminate in the triumph of liberal democracy.

BIBLIOGRAPHY

Abercrombie N, Hill S, and Turner BS: *Dominant Ideologies*. Unwin Hyman. 1990.

Aristotle: *Nichomachean Ethics*. Trans. JAK Thomson. Penguin. 1955.

____: *The Politics*. (Ca. 330 BCE) Trans. Ernest Barker. Oxford University Press. 1958.

Ayer, AJ *et. al.*: *What I Believe*. George Allen & Unwin. 1966.

Bannerman, Patrick: *Islam in Perspective*. Routledge and Kegan Paul. 1988.

Barrow, Robin: *Plato, Utilitarianism and Education*. Routledge and Kegan Paul. 1975.

Bell, Daniel: *The End of Ideology*. The Free Press. 1960.

Bentham, Jeremy: *Anarchical Fallacies* (1776) in *Bentham's Political Thought*. Barnes and Noble. 1973.

Bellamy, Richard: *Victorian Liberalism - Nineteenth-Century Political Thought and Practice*. Routledge and Kegan Paul. 1990.

Berlin, Isaiah: *Karl Marx: His Life and Environment*. Oxford University Press. 1939.

____: *The Age of Enlightenment*. The New American Library. 1956.

____: *Four Essays on Liberty*. Oxford University Press. 1969.

____: *Vico and Herder*. Hogarth Press. 1976.

____: *Russian Thinkers*. The Hogarth Press. 1978.

____: *Concepts and Categories*. Oxford University Press. 1939.

____: *Against the Current:Essays in the History of Ideas*. Oxford University Press. 1981.

____: *The Crooked Timber of Humanity*. Knopf. 1991.

Blackham, HJ: *Six Existentialist Thinkers*. Routledge & Kegan Paul. 1952.

Blinkhorn, Martin (Ed.): *Fascists and Conservatives*. Unwin Hyman. 1990.

Brown, LB: *Ideology*. Penguin. 1973.

Bull, Hedley: *The Anarchical Society*. Macmillan Press, 1977.

Cohen, GA: *Karl Marx's Theory of History: A Defence*. Clarendon Press. 1978.

Cooper, Barry: *The End of History: An Essay on Modern Hegelianism*. University of Toronto Press. 1943.

Cranston, Maurice: *Sartre*. Oliver and Boyd. 1962.

Crick, Bernard: *In Defence of Politics*. Weidenfeld & Nicolson. 1962.

Christenson, Alan *et. al: Ideologies and Modern Politics*. Nelson University. 1972.

Cruise O'Brien, Conor: *The Siege*. Paladin. 1986.

____: *Passion and Cunning and Other Essays*. Paladin. 1990.

Dahl, Robert A: *Polyarchy*. Yale University Press. 1979.

De Crespigny, Anthony: "Power and Its Forms" in De Crespigny and Wertheimer (Eds). 1970.

De Crespigny, A and Wertheimer A (Eds): *Contemporary Political Theory*. Nelson. 1970.

De Crespigny, A and Cronin, J (Eds): *Ideologies of Politics.* Oxford University Press. 1975.

De Crespigny, Anthony and Minogue, Kenneth: *Contemporary Political Philosophers.* Methuen . 1976.

Dunn, John: *Western Political Theory in the Face of the Future.* Cambridge University Press. 1979.

Du Preez, Peter: *The Politics of Identity.* Basil Blackwell. 1980.

Dworkin, Ronald: *Taking Rights Seriously.* Harvard University Press. 1978.

____: *Law's Empire.* Fontana Press. 1986.

____: "Liberalism", in Hampshire (Ed). 1978.

Fishkin, James S: *Justice, Equal Opportunity and the Family.* Yale University Press. 1983.

Flew, Antony: *The Politics of Procrustes.* Prometheus Books. 1981.

Friedrich, Carl J: *Constitutional Government and Democracy.* Ginn & Company. 1950.

Friedman, Milton and Rose: *Free to Choose.* Harmondsworth Penguin. 1980.

Fromm, Erich: *Marx's Concept of Man.* F Ungar. 1966.

Fukuyama, Francis: "The End of History?" in *The National Interest.* Summer. 1989.

____: "The End of History Debate" in *The National Inquirer.* Winter. 1989/90.

____: *The End of History and The Last Man.* Free Press. 1992.

Gellner, Ernest: *Thought And Change.* Weidenfeld & Nicolson. 1964.

____: *Nations and Nationalism.* Basil Blackwell. 1983.

____: *Spectacles and Predicaments.* Cambridge University Press. 1979.

Geras, Norman: "The Controversy about Marx and Justice" in *Philosophica 33.* 1984

Giddens, Anthony: *Modernity and Self-Identity.* Cambridge University Press. 1991

Glazer, N and Moynihan DP (Eds.): *Ethnicity.* Harvard University Press. 1975.

Graham, Gordon: "Religion and Politics" in *Philosophy.* 1983.

____: *Politics In Its Place.* Clarendon Press. 1986.

Hagopian, Mark N: *Ideals and Ideologies of Modern Politics.* Longman, 1985.

Hampshire, Stuart (Ed): *Public and Private Morality.* Cambridge University Press. 1978.

____: *Freedom of Mind.* (2nd Ed.) Chatto and Windus. 1975

____: *Thought and Action.* (New Edition) Chatto and Windus. 1982.

Hare, RM: *Moral Thinking.* Oxford University Press. (New Edition) 1982.

Hart, HLA: "Between Utility and Rights" in *Columbia Law Review,* 79 (1979) pp. 828-846.

____: *Essays on Bentham.* Clarendon Press. 1982.

Hart, HLA and Honore, Tony: *Causation and the Law.* (Revised Edition.) Oxford University Press. 1985.

Hayek, FA.: *The Constitution of Liberty.* Routledge and Kegan Paul. 1960.

____: *Law, Legislation and Liberty.* (3 Vols.) Routledge and Kegan Paul. 1973.

____: *New Studies in Philosophy, Politics, Economics and the History of Ideas.* Routledge and Kegan Paul. 1978.

Hegel, Georg Wilhelm Friedrich: *Phenomenology of Spirit.* (1807). Trans. AV Miller. Oxford University Press. 1977.

____: *The Philosophy of History.* (Ca. 1820) Trans. J Sibree. Dover Publications. 1956.

Hobbes, Thomas: *Leviathan.* (1651) Collier-Macmillan. 1969.

Illich, Ivan: *Deschooling Society.* Harmondsworth Penguin. 1970.

____: *Medical Nemesis.* Calder and Boyars. 1975.

Julian of Norwich: *The Revelations of Divine Love.* (Ca. 1393.) Penguin. 1966.

Kant, Immanuel: *Kant's Political Writings.* Ed. HS Reiss. Cambridge University Press. 1977.

Kedourie, Elie: *Nationalism.* Hutchinson. 1966.

Kolakowski, Leszek: *Main Currents in Marxism.* (3 Vols.) Trans. PS Falla. Clarendon Press.1978.

Letwin, William (Ed): *Against Equality.* Macmillan. 1983.

Lijphart, Arend: *Democracy in Plural Societies.* Yale University Press, 1977.

Lively, Jack: *Democracy.* Blackwell. 1984.

Locke, John: *Two Treatises of Government.* (1689) Ed. Peter Laslett. Cambridge University Press. (2nd Ed) 1967.

Lukes, Steven: *Marxism and Morality.* Oxford. 1985.

MacIntyre, Alasdair: *A Short History of Ethics.* Routledge and Kegan Paul. 1967.

____: *Against The Self-Images of the Age.* Duckworth. 1971.

____: *After Virtue*. University of Notre Dame Press. (Second Edition.) 1984.

____: *Whose Justice? Which Rationality?* Duckworth. 1988.

Macpherson, CB: *The Political Theory of Possessive Individualism*. Clarendon Press. 1973.

____: *The Real World of Democracy*. Oxford University Press. 1977.

____: *The Life and Times of Liberal Democracy*. Oxford University Press. 1977.

Machiavelli, N: *The Prince* and *Discourses on the First Decade of Livy's History in Political Writings*. (1516 and 1519.) Trans. Bruce Penman. JM Dent and Sons. 1981.

Magee, Bryan: *Men of Ideas*. Oxford University Press, 1982.

Mannheim, Karl: *Ideology and Utopia*. Trans. Louis Wirth and Edward Shils. University of Chicago Press. 1936.

Marcuse, Herbert: *One Dimensional Man*. Sphere Books. 1964.

Marx, Karl: *Capital* (1867). Allen and Unwin, 1938

____: *Selected Writings*. (Ed. David Mclellan) Oxford University Press. 1977.

Mill, John Stuart: *Utilitarianism*. (1861) *On Liberty*. (1859) *Representative Government*. (1861) (Everyman Edition.) JM Dent and Sons. 1910.

Minogue, Kenneth: *Nationalism*. Methuen. 1969.

Nozick, Robert: *Anarchy, State and Utopia*. Oxford University Press. 1974.

____: *Philosophical Explanations*. Clarendon Press. 1981.

Oakeshott, Michael: *Rationalism in Politics and Other Essays*. Methuen. 1956.

____: *On Human Conduct*. Clarendon Press. 1975.

____: *Hobbes on Civil Society*. Basil Blackwell. 1975.

____: *On History and Other Essays*. Basil Blackwell. 1983.

Orwell, George: *Collected Essays*. (2nd Ed.) Secker and Warburg. 1961.

Parekh, Bhiku. *Contemporary Political Thinkers*. Martin Robertson. 1982.

Parkinson, C Northcote: *Parkinson's Law*. Harmondsworth Penguin. 1955.

Pateman, Carole: *The Problem of Political Obligation*. Polity
Press. 1979.

Plato: *The Republic*. (Ca. 380 BCE) Trans. HPD Lee. Penguin. 1955.

Popper, Karl: *The Logic of Scientific Discovery*. (6th Impression Revised).
Hutchinson. 1972

____: *The Open Society and Its Enemies (*2 Vols. 5th Ed.) Routledge and
Kegan Paul.

____: *The Poverty of Historicism*. Routledge and Kegan Paul. 1957.

____: *Conjectures and Refutations*. (Second Edition.) Routledge and Kegan
Paul. 1965.

Postman, Neil: *Amusing Ourselves to Death*. Viking Penguin. 1985.

Proudhon P-J: *General Idea of the Revolution in France*. Trans.
JB Robinson. Freedom House. 1923.

Quinton (Ed): *Oxford Readings in Political Philosophy*. Oxford University
Press. 1967.

Rawls, John: *A Theory of Justice*. Cambridge. 1971.

Rousseau J-J: *Discourse on Inequality* (1755) and *The Social Contract*.
(1762). Trans. CE Vaughan. Cambridge University Press. 1915.

Ryan, Alan: *The Philosophy of Social Explanation*. Oxford University Press. 1973.

_____: *The Idea Of Freedom.* Oxford University Press. 1979.

_____: *Property and Political Theory*. Basil Blackwell. 1984.

Sartori, Giovanni: *Democratic Theory*. Frederick A Praeger Publishers. 1965.

Sartre J-P: *Existentialism is a Humanism.* Trans. Philip Miaret. Methuen. 1948.
_____: *Sartre par lui-meme.* Compiled by F Jeanson. Seuil. 1954.

Schaar, John H.: "Equality of Opportunity" in De Crespigny and Wertheimer (eds). 1970.

Schumpeter, Joseph: *Capitalism, Socialism and Democracy.* Allen and Unwin. 1943.

Stockman, David: *The Triumph of Politics*. Harper Collins. 1986.

Taylor, Charles: *Hegel.* Cambridge University Press. 1975.

Ward, J Neville: *The Use of Praying,* Epworth Press. 1967.

Williams, Bernard: *Moral Luck*. Cambridge University Press. 1981.

Williams, Howard: *Kant's Political Philosophy.* Basil Blackwell. 1983.

Woodcock, George: *The Anarchist Reader*. Fontana Press. 1977.

Wootton, Barbara: *What I Believe,* in Ayer *et. al.* 1966

INDEX